3-6-74

Some of My
Best Friends
Are
Christians

Books by Paul Blanshard

An Outline of the British Labor Movement
What's the Matter with New York (with Norman Thomas)
Investigating City Government
Democracy and Empire in the Caribbean
American Freedom and Catholic Power
Communism, Democracy and Catholic Power
The Right To Read
The Irish and Catholic Power
God and Man in Washington
Freedom and Catholic Power in Spain and Portugal
Religion and the Schools: The Great Controversy
Paul Blanshard on Vatican II
Personal and Controversial: An Autobiography
Some of My Best Friends Are Christians

Some of My Best Friends Are Christians

Paul Blanshard

Open Court
La Salle, Illinois

Printed in the United States of America
ISBN: 0-87548-149-3

Blanshard, Paul, 1892-
  Some of my best friends are Christians.

  Bibliography: p.
  1. Christianity—Controversial literature.
I. Title.
BL2775.2.B53   230   74-744

1823631

Contents

My trade is to say what I think
—Voltaire

*Some of My
Best Friends
Are
Christians*

Introduction

This is a very strange kind of book, and I think I should begin by describing just how it was born and how it differs from most books about religion.

Fifty-seven years ago I was a young preacher serving as pastor of the First Congregational Church of Tampa. (I have described that experience in my recent autobiography, *Personal and Controversial.*) I preached, prayed, married people, buried people, and tried to comfort the sick and the dying. I appealed glibly to the will of God. As preachers go I was not unsuccessful, but even after training in good seminaries and ordination I did not feel comfortable in the pulpit. I began to have devastating doubts about the truth of Christianity. I asked myself: Am I a liar for profit and prestige? Am I giving my people the conventional legends about God, Jesus, the Bible and death for their own comfort because that is the easy thing to do?

It was not the church as such that worried me. I believed in churches as centers of moral discussion and personal service. It was the *gospel* which I was supposed to preach. It was particularly agonizing at Easter time when I felt obliged to pretend that Jesus had actually risen from the dead and might possibly return to this world. What an improbable fairy story! And what a hypocrite I was when I blandly guaranteed immortality at funerals over the coffins of the dead!

That, at least, is how I began to think of myself as my doubts increased. I plunged into a heavy schedule of independent reading and soon discovered many new facts which had been excluded from my seminary studies. I came to feel that the whole fabric of Christian dogma was full of elementary delusions.

Finally, for my own satisfaction as much as anything, I sat down in 1917 and wrote a series of private essays or articles expressing my misgivings. When I began to write I never intended to have them published, and in fact they never were published under my own name. I called my collection of ruminations "The Immoral Reflections of a Preacher"—a rather inappropriate title since they contained no revelations of secret sin. They represented simply agonized doubt and youthful, rather naive, groping after truth.

When I had finished the articles—there were six—I obeyed a whimsical impulse, wrote the pseudonym "John Denmark" on the title page, and sent them off to Paul Carus, the distinguished editor of *The Open Court*, one of the most advanced intellectual magazines of that period. To my surprise, Carus accepted them and four of them were published between 1918 and 1920, but the war prevented publication in book form.

Now, 57 years later, Open Court Publishing Company has suggested that these articles might be the basis of a short book describing the long pilgrimage away from Christianity of one American. I accepted the publisher's suggestion with alacrity. Here is the result. My young ruminations are incorporated only as springboards for more extensive analyses written in 1974.

In a sense this book has become a bridge across the years, a long-distance dialogue with myself in which the speaking parts are separated in time by 57 years. To distinguish between the Paul Blanshard of 1917 and the Paul Blanshard of 1974 I have indicated where appropriate (Young Self—1917) or (Old Self—1974). It will be seen that there is much more of Old Self than of Young Self, and this is only natural because the world has moved a long way in the past 57 years, and I have moved far from the uneasy skepticism of my youth to the settled unbelief of my mature years.

I have not felt obliged to observe the concept of a balance between Young and Old Selves. Like Voltaire, I write as I please. With such license, I have written a long independent chapter on "Christianity and Sex," and here and there I break through the dialogue pattern in other ways. But I am keeping all the material that my Young Self wrote because I think he is an interesting period piece in skepticism: He had the courage of his convictions even if some of them seem extreme; and he was not any more extreme then than I am today. The changing attitude of the world toward orthodox Christianity has made the convictions of both Young Self and Old Self seem much less revolutionary than they seemed in 1917.

The articles I wrote in 1917 marked my exit from the Christian pulpit, not because I renounced churches but because I wanted to be honest. I had inherited the pulpit because both my father and grandfather had been clergymen. I chucked my heritage when I outgrew my Christianity.

I ask you, Gentle Reader, to approach the material in these pages with an open mind. That seems trite these days when open-mindedness is heralded as one of our most common virtues. Open-mindedness, however, is not considered a basic virtue in the field of organized religion. The most popular virtue in that field is something called faith. Tertullian boasted, "I believe because it is absurd." Many a Christian, who practices his faith as a kind of self-hypnosis, belongs in Tertullian's company.

The word "faith" is so important in my analysis that it needs to be examined. It is used—and misused—lavishly by both politicians and preachers. When a political orator uses it in the last paragraph of an after-dinner speech, just after he has mentioned the flag, he means not only loyalty to God but loyalty to himself, the President (if he belongs to the same party), the war machine, and the socalled democratic system. When an evangelist shouts the word across the uplifted faces of twenty thousand followers at a revival meeting, he usually means general acceptance of the Protestant brand of salvation. When the Pope intones the word in a jubilee prayer, he includes by inference obedience to himself and loyalty to the whole papal apparatus.

So faith is a thing of many-splendored meanings: confidence, loyalty, obedience, credulity, depending on the way it is used. I would ask you also, Gentle Reader, to suspend the operation of your faith as credulity and substitute therefor an honest and inquiring mind. Over-belief can be as damaging as outright lying, as the history of the Crusades and the Inquisition proves. Allegiance to truth is a virtue far superior to faith. I ask you in the name of truth to abandon sentimental predilections and read these pages without preconceptions.

You may ask why I should dedicate my energy to down-grading something which has so much good in it as Christianity. You may ask: Suppose it is true that Christianity has many archaic shortcomings, isn't it also true that it has so much of love and idealism in it that its shortcomings should be passed over?

My answer is negative because our culture is all of one piece. Religion is concerned with virtues and vices which affect the whole of life. When men promote illusions about gods, miracles and morals, their capacity for honesty is impaired in the fields of politics, education, business and family life. You cannot isolate the ill effects of hypocrisy. A corrupt religious society helps to corrupt secular society. And, as these pages will try to demonstrate, our dominant religious organization today is intellectually one of the least reputable things in our society. A heavy sugar-coating of humanitarianism cannot conceal that fact.

The manager of a wrecking crew does not have a pleasant job. His business is to tear things down so that better things can be built on new foundations. Some of the things he destroys have beauty and value. But there comes a time in the history of both cities and religions when the wrecking crew is necessary.

I believe that that time has come in the history of Western Christianity. The world of scholarship long ago revealed the decayed underpinning of Christian orthodoxy, but the clerical caretakers of the ancient temple still attempt to keep archaic beliefs alive with half-truths and irrelevant sentiments. Sooner or later there must be a reckoning between such Christianity and modern knowledge. Why not now?

Paul Blanshard
New Haven, Conn.

1 A Religious
Santa Claus

(Young Self—1917)

I sat down at the pipe-organ in my church last
night and played "More about Jesus." We sang
the song lustily—the choir was gathered
around me—and ended up with a glow of
satisfaction. It is a good song for young
throats and a good song for the pipe-organ. It
is more than that. Its central theme is the aim
of all those who are searching for the truth
about Christianity.

There can be no doubt what most men

A Religious Santa Claus

think concerning Jesus. Here in our Western civilization he is the Ideal of morality and faith. About him are clustered all the tender associations of religious devotion and unselfish service. To be Christlike is the highest goal of religious and moral growth; that has been my teaching and the teaching of millions of other religious men reared in Christian homes. The admiration for Jesus is evident not only in the church but in the labor union, the anarchist hall, the army and the saloon. Never has a name stood so high in the affection of men as the name of Jesus.

So a candid examination of Jesus is a delicate and dangerous thing. When Barnum said that the American public likes to be fooled, he might have added that we all hate the man who disillusions us about any favorite belief. We persist in misunderstanding him although his meaning may be as clear as sunlight.

Now I might be described, as to my morality, as the very essence of a "Christian gentleman." Perhaps I have been better than ordinary. I have never taken the name of God in vain, consumed so much as a mouthful of intoxicating liquor, stolen anything bigger than a street-car nickel, or gone the way of the brothel. I was looked upon in my youth as a model Sunday-school boy, and I still have that general reputation.

But Jesus Christ is not my ideal and never

will be. I am going to put down here why that is true.

When I was a child, Jesus was for me the Great Magician who stilled the waters, healed the sick, and made the blind to see. He was a great and perfect god, just as good a god as anybody wanted anywhere, and to disbelieve in this fact would bring my soul into danger of eternal damnation. Jesus was my religious Santa Claus.

When the time for disillusionment came, and Santa Claus and my parents lost their halos, the figure of Jesus was still untouched. My Sunday-school teachers at sixteen said the same things about Jesus that my Sunday-school teachers in the kindergarten had said.

In my university life the rude attacks of philosophy and higher criticism upon religion shook me profoundly, but these attacks were not directed against Jesus. I soon found that the professor who dared to make an open and frank criticism of Jesus in the classroom did not exist even in the state university. The professor handled Nero, Napoleon and Mohammed without gloves. Jesus of Nazareth who was said to be the greatest single force in history was carefully left to the discussion of the clergy.

So I emerged from the university with my picture of Jesus only slightly marred. Plunging into the studies of a theological seminary, I found that my professors did not believe in

Jesus in the same way that I did. Now, I thought, I will find out for myself what Jesus really means to the world. What is the secret of his tremendous influence over men?

My first critical study of the Gospels gave me a new Jesus. I had dreamed of a magician. When I looked into the Bible with care I found a prophet of rare passion and force, but a man ignorant and superstitious. The Jesus who stepped out of the pages of the New Testament to greet me was a towering and twisted figure, magnetic in his power but surrounded by all sorts of foolish traditions that were obviously as groundless as those traditions that held Buddhists and Mohammedans in their thralldom of ignorance. I found that there is no proof for a single miracle in the Old Testament or the New. Yet it is perfectly evident that the greatest part of the Jesus-power in the early growth of Christianity was due to the carefully nurtured belief that he had magic powers out of all proportion to the power of any other prophet or leader.

The leaders of our theological seminaries know that there is no proof for any of Jesus' miracles that would be considered acceptable for proving Mohammed's miracles, but they carefully avoid stating this fact in such a way that the people and the students can understand. Everywhere I have found a conspiracy of silence not only in regard to the miracles of Jesus but in regard to the other indefensible traditions that have grown up around him. The business of the theological school is to produce Christian ministers, and the rebel who questions the foundation of Christianity while he is in the seminary is like the soldier who announces his disloyalty to the flag after he has marched to the battlefield. On the battlefield

> "Theirs not to reason why:
> Theirs but to do and die."

I died. That is, my conscience was forgotten in the roar of battle. I shoved my real self aside in order to accomplish results. I followed the religious flag of my fathers because I was eager to be up and doing while youth and strength were mine.

Plunging into the work of a great city parish I found that the condition of the clerical mind concerning Jesus was even more chaotic than that of the student's mind. Barrels of sermons were preached on the perfection of the character and teachings of Jesus by men who never would dream of following in his way for a single day. Nowhere outside of the small group of Unitarian leaders did I find ministers who frankly asked themselves: is this declaration of Jesus true? If not, how can I preach him as an ideal? I noticed that the questions concerning the divinity or deity of Jesus were cleverly evaded by the more intelligent pastors. "Jesus is our great leader," they said, "and the test of our worth in the Father's sight is determined by our faithfulness in following him."

I believe that the almost universal dishonesty

about Jesus among the clergy is not at all deliberate. The preacher is usually as honest as the average lawyer or advertiser; he will interpret truth according to the visible results of his labor. If his preaching of Jesus is effective in winning members to his church and making them upright morally, he will go on preaching in the old way. It probably never occurs to him that other causes may be operating to bring the success of Christianity besides its truth. He does not realize that perhaps the most effective sermons for an ignorant congregation are the most untrue. So he leaves unasked the most rudimentary questions about Jesus: "If Jesus was the embodiment of God, why did he make so many mistakes? Why did he think and preach that the world was coming to an end within one generation? Why did he not leave us more clear and definite statements of the will of God? Why did he not save the world about 30 A.D. by making the supremacy of his moral law known?"

In confronting such questions as these, the average minister resorts to the refuge of agnosticism. We do not know the ways and the aims of God. God never intended man to know all these things. So we do not necessarily have to answer "foolish questions."

The continued emphasis upon faith as superior to reason has had its effect. It is now possible for the religious man to pass over the most fundamental and searching questions in regard to Christianity without analysis by the simple assertion, "we cannot understand all the mysteries of the incarnation of God's spirit in Jesus Christ, but we know from experience that it is a fact."

To which the opponent of Christianity makes reply: "What do we know about Jesus Christ from experience?"

He was a Jew who lived almost two thousand years ago. He spoke a language which would be utterly unintelligible to us today. He never wrote anything that would give us an exact idea of his teaching and personality. We do not know what he looked like, when he was born, or when he died. What we know about his life is summed up in badly jumbled conjecture written in a language he did not speak, by men some of whom he never saw. Only three of the thirty-three or more years of his life are known to us and our accounts of those three years differ widely. Outside of the few faithful followers who held firm to the end, Jesus made no lasting impression upon the people of his time. We are asked to reject the judgment of the whole world of Jesus' time, which stamped him as an unimportant preacher, and accept the estimate of those who followed him as a God, a Magician, and a Prophet.

The opponent of Christianity insists that we do not know enough about the historical Jesus to worship him or follow him with any enthusiasm or certainty. The perfection of his character and the power of his magic healing cannot be a part of our experience because we are not sure that they ever existed. They are a part of Christian tradition and nothing more. The Jesus who flits across the stage of the New Testament, loving, praying, cursing and healing is quite too vague in his outlines to convey any clear picture to us.

Common sense will tell us that when a figure is so dim as that of the historical Jesus there is a great temptation to appropriate the figure for the advancement of all varieties of reform. The human race likes to dream of idols and then find an idol to fit the dream. Jesus has become the Great Dream Prophet of the Western world because there have clustered about him the yearnings and imaginings of a credulous race. So we have virtually created a "Christ" who bears the relation to the historical Jesus that the personality of the real "Santa Claus" bears to the personality of our father.

Jesus has been identified with an Ideal Dream because the mystery surrounding his life gives room for the free play of imagination. If our Santa Claus were dressed in a blue shirt and overalls he would be a ridiculous failure. There would be no romance about him. So we take our Christ from a land on the other side of the world where customs and traditions allow these magic fringings that are so necessary to stimulate the imagination. Palestine and the Jews will not worship with us at Bethlehem, for they know Bethlehem too well . . .

When modern scholarship tore away the grave-clothes from the buried Jesus, men began to see the difference between the dream and the reality. A wave of acute Unitarianism swept the country. Then dream-loving human nature reasserted itself and "reconciled" the Christ ideal with the spirit of Jesus by carefully culling out the ideal from the superstitious. But the task has not been well done. The patchwork shows.

Two-thirds of the people of America are outside the church partially because they feel that Jesus does not really save them. They feel that the personality of Jesus will not stretch to the dimensions of an omnipotent Christ.

The reasons why we cannot maintain the old devotion to Jesus become clear when we analyze the records in our possession and ask two leading questions.

Is Jesus as he is sketched in the New Testament sufficiently compelling to command our worship of him as a perfect leader? Are his chief teachings as recorded in the New Testament fundamentally true?

Jesus the Magician is so near the front of the stage at all times in the New Testament narrative that we can scarcely extricate Jesus the Man. We judge, however, that he was kind and benevolent, for he loved little children and expressed great anxiety for the hungry multitudes who followed him. He liked to describe himself as the Good Shepherd, and his people were evidently struck with the aptness of the description. He must have been exceedingly brave. He defied the Pharisees in their own haunts and stood before Pilate with all the self-mastery of a Stoic. His large audiences, won without any political prestige to aid him, show that he was a powerful personality with splendid oratorical powers. His vitriolic denunciation of the Pharisees and his wrathful attack upon the money-changers in the Temple reveal a man of impulsive anger. His habits of dining with publicans and sinners and of working with poor folks showed that he was a leader who had genuine sympathies for the masses of men.

Beyond these few qualities, sketchily revealed, what do we know of the personality of Jesus? His boyhood and youth are a blank. (The story of his boyhood revelations of wisdom in the Temple is almost undoubtedly a legend like all the other legends of childhood miracles that have grown up about religious leaders of the East.) We do not even know whether Jesus had the respect of his neighbors as an upright workman. Nazareth did not recognize his ability, for he was driven from the streets when he did not perform a miracle in his own city.

During his ministry Jesus showed practically no knowledge that it would not be possible to gain in an ordinary Galilean town. He makes no reference to any of the great Greek thinkers who had lived before him. He made no attempt, so far as we know, to record his teachings in a clear and forceful way.

The personality of Jesus can be better understood by comparison with any ancient or modern religious leader. There is a peculiar sameness about all the world's great religious leaders in spite of the efforts of the disciples of each to prove the uniqueness of their favorite.

Buddha, for instance, was miraculously conceived and sent forth into the world to preach a gospel of world renunciation and unselfishness. He came from a very wealthy and powerful family, was converted to his new faith by divine plan and spent the years of his long life preaching, organizing congregations, and serving mankind. The traditions that have grown up around Buddha have made him into an incarnation of the deity, yet there is no indication that he was anything more than a great teacher. His own religious enthusiasm and the admiration of his followers persuaded him to claim that he was the Perfect One.

The dreamy and superstitious mystics who made Buddha into a Perfect One were not very different from the people who initiated Christianity. The founders of Christianity may have been respected artisans in their various homes, but they were no more intelligent in the science of universal thinking than the inhabitants of the mountains of Tennessee. When we see how easy it is in the modern scientific world to create a Joseph Smith or a Mary Baker Eddy, the power of superstition in the days of almost universal illiteracy can be realized. Religious enthusiasm as it applies to leaders is one of the most undiscerning forces in the world. Even love cannot be so blind.

But the Jesus of the New Testament has an irresistible charm about him which all the delusions of his followers and all the quarreling schools of theologians have not entirely destroyed. As a god he is personally vain and intellectually inadequate. As a passionate, daring and hot-headed evangelist he appeals to the virility of all men. He shows that inimitable genius for hearty, democratic fellowship which made him the idol of common folk. He was no half-way prophet: He was no truckler to the rich. He loved the oppressed as much as he hated the oppressor. In him there were combined something of that tenderness and battle lust which have commanded the loyalty of men in every age.

The personality of Jesus will continue to move men long after organized Christianity has lost its power.

We cannot call him perfect, for he was at times harsh and haughty, at times provincial and ignorant, and at times inordinately vain. We cannot call him God, for every fact of modern science and the now generally accepted theory of evolution make it impossible that the infinite, progressive Force of the Universe should have been entirely expressed in a Palestinian Jew who lived hundreds of years ago. But Jesus had that invincible determination to speak the truth and that unflinching courage of the martyr which will always make him a leader of magnetic power. The chief controversies of recent years have centered around the teachings of Jesus rather than his personality. What can we accept and what must we reject in those teachings?

I believe that the chief sin of the clergy is refusing to define for themselves and their congregations the part of Jesus' teachings which they *cannot* accept. We would not call a man a good follower of Mohammed if he rejected three-fourths of the prophet's leading teachings and accepted only that which accorded with his own ideas of what a religion should be. Yet that is precisely what the American clergy is doing with the teachings of Jesus.

In my last reading of the Gospels I noted how much of Jesus' time was consumed in preaching about the coming of the kingdom of God. The ideal he held before men was a worthy one, but we cannot honestly believe in it today. Jesus believed in a kingdom which was coming almost *immediately*, a kingdom whose coming should be preceded by a terrible judgment day in which his followers should be weeded out from all the unbelievers among men and exalted to the throne of God. The conviction of the early coming of that kingdom is apparent in every sermon that Jesus preached and in the interpretation put upon his Gospel by all his disciples from John the Baptist to Paul. "And there shall be signs in the sun, and in the moon, and in the stars; and upon earth distress of nations, with perplexity; the sea and the waves roaring ... Verily I say unto you, This generation shall not pass away, till all be fulfilled" (Luke 21).

"For as the lightning cometh out of the east, and shineth even to the west; so shall also the coming of the Son of man be ... Immediately after the tribulation of those days shall the sun be darkened, and the moon shall not give her light, and the stars shall fall from heaven, and the powers of the heavens shall be shaken: and then shall appear the sign of the Son of man in heaven: and then shall all the tribes of the earth mourn, and they shall see the Son of Man coming in the clouds of heaven with power and great glory. And he shall send his angels with a great sound of a trumpet, and they shall gather together his elect from the four winds, from one end of heaven to the other.

"Now learn a parable of the fig tree; When his branch is yet tender, and putteth forth leaves, ye know that summer is nigh: So likewise ye, when ye shall see all these things, know that it is near, even at the doors. VERILY I SAY UNTO YOU, THIS GENERATION SHALL NOT PASS TILL ALL THESE THINGS BE FULFILLED" (Matt. 24).

Modern teachers have glossed over the

words of Jesus concerning the kingdom and made it seem that he intended a kingdom of justice and righteousness here upon earth, and nothing more. But Jesus had a very different ideal in mind. He definitely predicted again and again a *physical* kingdom here upon earth which should be accomplished by a miraculous disruption of nature by the hand of God. We cannot identify the kingdom of moral life which we seek to establish through personal and social reconstruction with the star-falling-cloud-charioted arrival of Jesus.

We know now that Jesus was wrong when he predicted that the world would come to a cataclysmic end within one generation, but preachers still attribute to Jesus the intelligence which modern science has given them. They continually evade the plain and undeniable fact that Jesus was wrong in the chief doctrine of his Gospel. They denounce those street preachers and fanatics of all sorts who use the Bible to predict the early end of the world, when the truth is that those street preachers are maintaining the Gospel of Jesus in its purity more conscientiously than our leading theologians.

The fact that Jesus expected the early end of the world throws a new light upon all his ethical teachings. The morality of the last week of the world would necessarily be quite different from the morality of the three-millionth week in a series of 98,783,521,306 ... weeks. A man can quite readily love his neighbors if he knows that all their life interests and rivalries are to be wiped out in the next week, and they are both to become part of a kingdom of brotherhood. Such a man need "take no thought for the morrow." Such a man can turn the other cheek with the silent assurance: "My God will reward me for this goodness when I arrive in his kingdom next week. Why should I concern myself with anything but the saving of my own soul and the souls of my friends?"

So the Sermon on the Mount, which embodies some of the great moral ideals of the race, is quite impossible as a program of moral conduct in a world which may never end because it is inspired by the conviction· that the meek, the hungry, the persecuted and the sorrowful will be relieved of their troubles not by scientific betterment but by the supernatural charity of the coming kingdom. Reverse every one of the beatitudes and you have the moral code which rules our American business life, not because our business life is altogether horrible but because it is based on the assumption of permanence.

A more serious charge can be made against the teachings of Jesus than anything I have yet mentioned. We have come to believe in our modern life that we are saved by character rather than belief. It is not right that any man should be stamped with the approval of the gods merely because he accepts an explanation of life presented by someone else. A man's value to the world is generally measured by the amount of service he renders to the community.

The teachings of Jesus emphasize above everything else in the salvation of the race the acceptance of himself as Divine Savior. John does not say, "For God so loved the world that he sent to the world a great example of unselfish service that whosoever labored in his spirit should gain eternal life." Rather it is written, "For God so loved the world, that he gave his only begotten Son, that whosoever BELIEVETH in him should not perish but have everlasting life."

John 3:16 expresses the heart of Christianity. I am not one of those intellectual jugglers who try to dodge this point. And the experience of the human race shows that when we make salvation dependent upon the acceptance of facts concerning a religious personality, we undermine the very foundation of moral life. When I can be saved by believing right, there is no earthly use in doing right. When I allow theological views to be a condition of salvation I ignore those economic and social forces that really save people. I might think that Jesus was an imposter and a lunatic and that belief would not affect my salvation if I sincerely devoted myself to my own highest ideals.

I have never met a half-dozen men who seriously accepted the Christian standard of salvation, i.e., all men who reject the belief in

Jesus' unique sonship will be eternally damned and all men who accept will live eternally. The church has too much sense to accept it, so it adds on to the standard certain moral laws which entirely change its meaning. It is an abomination to intelligence to say that the living goodness of an active race was epitomized in an historical figure who lived two thousand years ago. Goodness is not a stagnant thing. It moves forward with the relentless progress of a juggernaut, and is so much bigger than the personality of Jesus or any prophet that it is hard to believe that some men still hold the old belief.

There is but one choice in this matter. If the goodness of mankind grows from century to century, then Jesus cannot be our infallible moral guide. Every principle of modern science points to the fact that mankind is going forward in the attempt to solve the great riddle of salvation, and that moral laws must not be bound down to any one personality. Personalities are but incidents in the growth of moral systems. Jesus may have given expression to the most sublime moral ideals of mankind but the truth of those ideals does not depend upon him.

The People and not any one Person shall teach me what to do. When religious leaders try to fasten my moral judgment to a teacher who lived many hundreds of years ago, they show complete ignorance of the nature of my moral decisions.

Jesus as an inspirer of unselfish conduct will always interest me. Jesus as a divine authority in conduct will stultify my conscience and make me a moral child.

The problem of Jesus and the salvation of the world is greatly complicated by teachers who make over Jesus to suit their ideals. Like a dreamer before a magic mirror Bernard Shaw has looked into the story of Christianity and beheld a Fabian economist born in Bethlehem. With the vivid coloring of a powerful imagination Bouck White in *The Call of the Carpenter* has put himself back into Judea. The pictorial power of these writers is so great that thousands have been convinced of the true modernness of Jesus.

Would that I too could be convinced. The Jesus of Bernard Shaw or Bouck White is infinitely more compelling than any prophet of the Scriptures. But the New Testament is too much for me.

The Jesus of the New Testament is distinctly a product of his time, and his time was ignorant and superstitious. If he gave an economic gospel to his time, his disciples never heard of it, and they saw much more of him than Bernard Shaw or Bouck White ever did. Jesus was known as the mystic, the dreamer, the prophet, the wonder-worker, but never as the master sociologist. How could his mind be occupied with the adjustment of society when that society was to end in an earthquake within the generation?

Palestine two thousand years ago could not have produced the master of sociology any more than the Stone Age could have produced Plato. Judea wanted a message of personal faith and salvation, and Jesus was sensitive enough and able enough to feel the need and supply the message. If he had spoken the thoughts of modern socialism or any kind of socialism, his people would have looked on in dumb stupidity. The real message of Jesus stands there in the New Testament, full of gross superstition and ignorance, forever damning the efforts of enthusiasts to make it over into a message of practical social reform.

For a long time the Church has been too sane to preach pure Christianity—I mean the teachings of Jesus in their entirety. We brush aside those teachings which the twentieth century cannot accept and preach those "essentials" which our time demands. Whatever we agree with is branded as essential to Jesus' teachings. The unthinking observer imagines that we are really preaching Christianity. We are preaching what we want to preach. *We* and not Jesus are the authorities of our moral teaching.

Many a critic standing on the outside of the church makes his mistake here. He imagines that the real strength of the church is based upon the teachings of Jesus. Listen to Nietzsche in this bitter attack:

"When on a Sunday morning we hear the old bells ringing, we ask ourselves: Is it possible? All this for a Jew crucified two thousand years ago who said he was God's son? The proof of such an assertion was lacking ... Certainly the Christian religion constitutes in our time a protruding bit of antiquity from very remote ages and that its assertions are still generally believed ... although men have become so keen in the scrutiny of claims ... constitutes the oldest relic of this inheritance. A god who begets children by a mortal woman; a sage who demands that no more work be done, that no more justice be administered but that the signs of the approaching end of the world be heeded; a system of justice that accepts an innocent as a vicarious sacrifice in the place of the guilty; a person who bids his disciples drink his blood; prayers for miracles; sins against a god expiated against a god; fear of a hereafter to which death is the portal; the figure of a cross as a symbol in an age that no longer knows the purpose and the ignominy of the cross—how ghostly all these things flit by before us out of the grave of their primitive antiquity! Is one to believe that such things can still be believed?"

The church bells of our own day do not mean that all these things are being taken seriously inside the churches. The preachers present their own moral views before the people and manage to discover a text from the Bible to hang their sermon upon with several ringing quotations for good measure. They use the name of Jesus to support their analysis of life in the same way that a politician uses the name of Lincoln in his peroration. The resemblance to Jesus is as marked as the resemblance of the average politician to the Great Emancipator.

There are many men (commonly called cynics) who see these truths but who refuse to attack the church or the personality of Jesus because they are bound up with everything that is ideal in our civilization.

"Of what importance is it to us," they ask, "that Jesus was not what the world believed him to be? His teachings are doing much good in the world and the churches are uplifting men in his name."

But how fatal it is to build a religion upon a fundamental fraud. If Jesus is not the actual savior of the world why should we face backward to a personality and teachings that the world has outgrown?

There cannot be two Christs in my life. If my conscience, alert and sensitive to modern needs, is to be my guide then the conscience of the Judean teacher can be of only reference value. And does not the advance of knowledge mean this, that in place of the rulership of popes and kings and Christs there shall be substituted the supremacy of a man's own moral reason?

My moral reason is my Christ and ever will be. In the light of that moral reason I meet Jesus of Nazareth as a peculiar and mysterious acquaintance. I am cordial in my admiration at those few times when our souls seem to find common ground. I sympathize with him in defeat and rejoice in his victories. I am thankful for the good things which he has given me and scornful of his almost insane egotism. Earnestly I listen to his words, for he is a fellow pilgrim on life's way.

Then I pass on to win salvation for myself.

2 How Christianity Was Manufactured

(Old Self—1974) 1823631

I think that most of the things I said about Jesus in the last chapter are as true in 1974 as they were then, but there is a great deal to be added if one is to understand how Christianity was manufactured. Christianity did not spring full-blown from the brow of Jesus or even from the brow of St. Paul, who had a great deal more to do with the manufacture of Christianity than Jesus himself. Christianity took about three hundred years to jell and when its creed finally took form at the Council of Nicea in 325 A.D., it did not look much like the simple millennial kingdom-dream that had been promoted by the young prophet from Galilee.

Christianity's growth has often been described as magical and divine. A study of its actual history indicates that its success was largely accidental. For a time several competing sects with equally plausible gospels seemed about to smother it. In the fourth century the competing Manichees seemed to have prospects for ruling the Mediterranean world and they were beaten down only by Christian strong-arm tactics. In the competition among sects, rationality seemed to have little to do with success. There was no clear distinction between superstition and reality. There were no newspapers, magazines and books to create an informed public opinion either about religion or any other phase of life. Printing was not to be invented for some thirteen centuries, and probably about 99 per cent of the people of Jesus' time were illiterate.

In the whole area of faith, power was monopolized by shamans, priests, prophets and fakirs who had no agreed standards of truth-telling and criticism. Jesus himself believed in demons and the devil and boasted that he had "cast out demons" (Luke 13:32). He talked to the devil on a mountain when he was tempted during his forty-day isolation (Matt. 4:1-11), and in the famous story of the Gaderene swine (Matt. 8: 28-33) he drove the demons out of the sickly and insane men into a herd of pigs and sent the poor pigs squealing down to their death in the sea.

Incidentally, Jesus was often vengeful and petty in his bursts of temper, and some of the things I said about his character in the last chapter should have this addendum. His language was often mixed heavily with anger and spite. He irascibly blighted a poor fig tree for all eternity (Matt. 21:19) because it had no ripe fruit for him when he went to pick some. He savagely condemned any city that rejected him: "It shall be more tolerable for the land of Sodom and Gomorrah in the day of judgment than for that city" (Matt. 10:15). He was far from kind to his own mother, perhaps because his mother was for a long time skeptical of his messianic claims. ("Woman what have I to do with thee?" John 2:4). Sometimes his parables produced a moral quite contrary to social justice, as, for example, the parable of the equal wages for those who worked a long and short work schedule (Matt. 20: 1-10). His claim to the role of peacemaker was somewhat clouded by his statement: "Think not that I came to send peace on the earth: I came not to send peace but a sword." (Matt. 10:34).

The manufacture of Christianity in the first

three hundred years was a hit-and-miss production partly because there was no Bible to guide the faithful. There was the Jewish Old Testament, of course, and that was the only gospel Jesus knew, but there was no New Testament, no bundle of Jesus' sermons, no biography of Jesus, not even a picture of him. All existing pictures are based on imagination and rumor. And for a long time there were no theological treatises to guide the faithful.

How could a religion like Christianity grow without a literature? The answer is that it could not grow intelligently or systematically. It emerged as a conglomeration of primitive hopes and fancies. The first-century Christians spent much time in quarreling over trivial things, especially the trivial ceremonial differences between Judaism and Gentile Christianity. Jesus' disciples were largely illiterate and if they had been able to read and write they could not have found any scholarly manuscript to tell them what was important and unimportant in the Master's teaching.

The contemporary writers of the non-Christian world were completely silent in their treatment of the young prophet of Nazareth. Apparently no contemporary Roman or Greek historian considered him and his movement worth mentioning. Tacitus and the younger Pliny mentioned him briefly but they were not contemporaries. (Tacitus, in mentioning Christianity, said that "this name was given to it from one Christus, who in the reign of Tiberius had been condemned to death by the procurator Pontius Pilate, so that the pestilent superstition was for the moment put down.") Josephus, the most prominent of the contemporary historians who might have been expected to say something about Jesus, said not a word. One famous passage about Jesus in Josephus' writings is now universally regarded as an interpolation.

When the New Testament canon finally did arrive about the middle of the fourth century, the accepted manuscripts constituted a strange mixture of earnest, incoherent and contradictory propaganda. Not a single book or paragraph in the New Testament was written in the only language which Jesus spoke, Aramaic. Not a single account of Jesus' life was written by an eye witness. The famous four Gospels, Matthew, Mark, Luke and John, were attributed to well-known disciples in order to acquire prestige. There never was a "harmony" of these four Gospels because they contained hundreds of contradictions and inconsistencies. The fourth Gospel, for example, the Gospel attributed to John, was a later addition to the three Synoptics, and it is now universally admitted that its theology is quite foreign to that of Matthew, Mark and Luke.

It is a harsh thing to say that the Gospels were forgeries because in these pre-scientific days there was no clear line between originality and forgery. Scribes copied and tinkered with the "original" without having any definite standard of originality. By strict literary standards, all of the three Synoptic Gospels are forgeries. That is to say, they are collections of overlapping accounts of parts of Jesus' life, laboriously copied by many hands in a pre-printing era, and changed as often as the various scribes wanted to establish a better story. There were no standards of scholarship to prevent plagiarism or alterations, no copyright office to prosecute for literary theft. If a local scribe, copying a manuscript laboriously by hand, wanted to improve on the text, he went ahead and improved, feeling pride in any new and interesting material he had added. So grew the sacred literature of Christianity which, many centuries later, was hailed by the Lutheran Church—Missouri Synod as accurate and inspired to the last comma by God Himself.

In this early, confused world of non-scholarship there were two factors which greatly affected the manufacture of Christianity. One I shall call the gap, and the other the mythological ethos.

The gap is the distance in time between the death of Jesus and the first writings which were finally accepted as parts of the canon of the New Testament. This gap was anywhere between twenty and a hundred twenty years, perhaps even more in some cases. Paul's epistles came before the four Gospels, so he should ordinarily be considered a more informed biographer than Matthew, Mark, Luke or John. But he was not. He did not present a real life of Jesus in his writings, and he omitted those magic tales about Jesus with which the four Gospels are filled. We do not even know to this day which books of the New Testament were written by Paul. There are allegedly fourteen epistles, but probably only four were written by Paul, perhaps ten.

The two words which most accurately describe the state of our knowledge about the New Testament are "perhaps" and "probably." Probably the four Gospels, garbled and contradictory as they are, represent with some accuracy what the devout followers believed between 70 and 100 A.D., but John is later and less reliable as a historical source than the three Synoptics, Matthew, Mark and Luke. Mark, considered the most authoritative of the Gospels, may perhaps be dated between 60 and 70 A.D., Matthew and Luke are drawn in part from an earlier and lost fragment called Q. Matthew came after Mark and the author of Luke probably wrote Acts. John, not the Apostle John, perhaps wrote about 110 A.D., perhaps much later. John's point of view is heavily philosophical, not seeming to belong with the rest of the New Testament. To add to the multiple uncertainties, nobody knows when Jesus was born or died. The Christmas date legend is just a beautiful legend, like the whole legend of the stable and of Bethlehem.

Perhaps Jesus was born in 7 B.C., perhaps later. Perhaps he died in 37 A.D., perhaps not. Probably he lived at some time; his existence in time is one of the few facts about him that now commands almost universal acceptance.

The gap between the death of Jesus and the appearance of his alleged biographies is not the most important flaw in Christian history. When the Gospels themselves are compared, it is clear that there are contradictions and inconsistencies in almost every chapter. The "authors" did not consult one another in order to eliminate contradictions. The earliest Greek manuscripts of the New Testament which we possess are made up of four thousand fragments, and they are said to contain about 150,000 discrepancies. The most famous discrepancy in the Gospels is the double genealogy of Jesus in Matthew 1 and Luke 3, tracing his ancestry through different generations down to Joseph, not to the Holy Spirit and the Virgin Mary.

Paul, although he never met Jesus, lived close enough to Jesus' time to produce a biography of him, but he never tried. After the famous conversion on the road to Damascus, Paul, instead of making a thorough inquiry into Jesus' life, disappeared for meditation in Arabia. "I conferred not with flesh and blood," he says in Galations 1:16. He did not want to take his Christianity from advisers. Apparently he knew nothing about the Virgin Birth or the Trinity.

In this age of sophistication and science we do not need to take seriously the New Testament catalogue of miracles produced by Jesus and the apostles. Many of these miracles were too absurd or too trivial to mention, and it is obvious that even the authors of the Gospels did not accept them. Their tales of these miracles differ sharply, and some of the most important are mentioned in one Gospel only. Mark does not mention Jesus' miraculous birth; Matthew and Luke tell conflicting stories about it; all the four Gospels manufacture differing tales about Jesus' resurrection; the story in Mark 16 about Jesus' many appearances after death is an obvious later interpolation. Jesus' chief miracle, the raising of Lazarus from the dead, is recorded only in John. And so on.

We know now that life in our solar system follows certain natural laws. These laws are not easily violated by magic-mongers who plead divine help. Such violations should not be accepted as fact by reasonable men unless there is overwhelming proof. We would be justified in saying with David Hume that "no testimony can prove miracles, for it is more probable that the testimony is false than that the miracles are true." But it is not necessary to go that far. We can say simply that miracles are unlikely, and that the fantastic New Testament miracles attributed to Jesus have no support from science or from any impartial historians or analysts. The incidents themselves are inherently incredible not only because they violate the laws of nature but because, if they had really happened, the whole Mediterranean world of Jesus' time would have been electrified by their magnitude.

If Jesus had actually raised Lazarus from the dead and kept him alive, if Jesus had actually walked on the waters, if Jesus had actually touched a blind man's eyes and made him see, if Jesus had actually risen from the dead and revealed himself to "many" witnesses, nothing could have prevented the rise of a great mass movement of on-the-spot devotees. But nothing like this happened. The Resurrection, allegedly the greatest event in all human history, was not attested by a single contemporary non-Christian writer, and the stories about the event in the New Testament are told with wavering inexactitude, full of contradictions and unverified rumors.

The second great factor of this early period which affected the manufacture of Christianity was what I have called the mythological ethos. The whole Middle Eastern area was saturated with religious mythology, much of it so strikingly similar that many of its authors could have been charged with plagiarism. Unbelievable religions were about as common as locusts. Each faith had its battery of gods and its supply of miracles. The Persians had Zoroaster, the Greeks Zeus, the Egyptians

Osiris, etc., etc. The stories about these gods and their kindred were shockingly like the legends concerning Yahweh and Jesus. Many of the Eastern gods known to Greece and Rome were gods who died and rose again, and virgin births for these gods were routine. One writer has produced a book called *The World's Sixteen Crucified Saviors*, claiming that there were actually twenty such claimants to the Christ role.

Many of these competing religions were semi-political in nature, tied up to state thrones and promoted by political dictators along with national patriotism. Often the god of a regional religion would be himself the local king, combining patriotism and prayer in fruitful partnership.

These local and national religions, of course, were very careless about truth, partly because there was no generally accepted standard of truth in religious matters. Almost all religions competed in producing incredible marvels, and both Judaism and Christianity joined in this competition. If Yahweh could stop the sun in front of Jericho, if a whale could swallow Jonah and keep him for three days, if Balaam's ass could speak, why could not Jesus raise Lazarus from the dead and afterwards rise himself? There was no board of scientific examiners to check the credentials of the competitors in myth-making. It was during this period of unrestrained rumor-mongering that Christianity rose from a small, feeble sect to become a state religion, and the tales of saints' bones and the golden wings of angels grew along with the trappings of political power.

Some Christian scholars who reject the miracles and who acknowledge the fact that Christianity has borrowed many myths from other religions still argue that there is in the New Testament enough of unique truth to make Christianity *the* moral religion. But is the moral teaching of Jesus so clear and convincing that it deserves superior ranking? It contains elements of great insight but as a total faith it is strangely deficient.

To begin with, the teachings of Jesus are not assembled coherently in any one place in the New Testament. There is the so-called Sermon on the Mount in the fifth chapter of Matthew, and similar fragments in the so-called sermon on the plain in the sixth chapter of Luke. But apparently these are nothing more than parabolic fragments assembled from various talks. Even the Lord's Prayer is not rendered in Matthew and Luke in identical language (Matt. 6 and Luke 11)—and the circumstances surrounding the prayer in the two Gospels are in conflict. The unsystematic character of Jesus' teaching was revealed unwittingly by Thomas Jefferson when he assembled what he called *The Life and Morals of Jesus of Nazareth.* The small book, full of beautiful sentiments, is so fragmentary in its summary that it could not serve as the cogent basis of any cogent religion.

Modern scholars are almost unanimous in

describing the Sermon on the Mount as a collection taken from many other discourses, not an organized or authoritative pronouncement of an ethical code for this world. If the beatitudes are closely examined, it will be seen that they are largely untrue. At least they are untrue for the world in which they were spoken, and just as untrue for our present world. Blessed are the meek for they shall inherit the earth. Where do they inherit the earth? Blessed are the merciful for they shall obtain mercy. Where? In Vietnam? In the Soviet Union? In Spain? In the Palestine of Jesus' time?

Whatever we may think of the sweeping moral generalizations of Jesus, it is clear that they were not proposed for an on-going world. Jesus did not say anything particularly important for his own day about slavery, war, racial oppression or poverty. He talked a temporary situation ethics for a temporary world which was soon destined to become a super-earthly kingdom. His prophecies and warnings about the future doom of man make this all too clear.

Although there is a sort of shining goodness in many of the utterances of Jesus, those utterances are scarcely original. The best of them, "Love thy neighbor as thyself," existed in its simplest form in Leviticus 19:18. Jesus never repudiated his debt to the Jewish prophets.

The more one studies the life of Jesus the

more one is forced toward a rather startling conclusion. Jesus was not a Christian. He was a reforming Jew who remained a reforming Jew to the end. He believed finally that he was the Messiah of the Jews, and he continued to worship the Jewish God and observe most of the Jewish law. Paul's Christianity was a post-Jesus Christianity, a religion about Jesus which finally triumphed over the religion of Jesus.

I have described this conclusion as rather startling but it is not new and it has been mulled over and debated for centuries by Christian and non-Christian scholars. It was essentially the view accepted by T. H. Huxley, the most brilliant of the anti-Christian pioneers of the last century. Voltaire in his rollicking story, *The Sage and the Atheist*, has Freind the philosopher say to the inquisitor: "Does it become you... to roast people alive because they are descended from a sect that formerly inherited a rocky canyon near the Syrian desert? What does it matter to you whether a man is circumcised or not? That he observe Easter at the full of the moon or on the following Sunday?... Do you know... that Jesus Christ was a Jew—that he was born, lived, and died a Jew? That he observed the passion like a Jew at the full of the moon? That all his apostles were Jews?"

Perhaps the most convincing defense of the thesis that Jesus was a Jew has been written by Professor Joseph Klausner of the Hebrew University in Jerusalem. In his two works, *Jesus of Nazareth* and *Jesus to Paul*, Klausner argues that "it did not even enter the mind of Jesus to form a new religion and proclaim it outside the Jewish nation. The Law and the Prophets—these were his faith and religion; the people of Israel—this was the people to whom this religion had been given as an inheritance and who must establish it in its fullness."

The final stage in the manufacture of Christianity came with the institution in Rome of a great centralized organization known as the Roman Catholic Church. It gave the scattered little assemblies of early Christians authority and discipline. After the conversion of the Emperor Constantine and the Edict of Milan in 313, Christianity achieved recognition as the state religion. The state obligingly suppressed competing heresies and built a structure of political and ecclesiastical power for the Church. Organized Christianity had arrived.

I cannot find anything in the teaching of Jesus to justify such an institution. It grew out of practical necessities, not out of any divine sanction. It rendered a great service to organized Christianity but its alleged biblical claim to divine origin is nothing but self-serving myth.

Surely if Jesus had intended to establish a great ecclesiastical machine as a Christian church he would have made his intention so clear that all the Gospels would have contained the directive. None of the Gospels contains such an unequivocal directive. Only one Gospel, Matthew, contains a broadly general, almost symbolic statement which the other three Gospels do not repeat. That statement reads: "Thou art Peter and upon this rock I will build my church; and the gates of hell shall not prevail against it. I will give unto thee the keys of the kingdom of heaven; and whosoever thou shalt bind on earth shall be bound in heaven; and whatsoever thou shalt loose on earth shall be loosed in heaven." (Matt. 16: 18-19)

This passage is almost certainly an interpolation since it is inconceivable that Jesus should have considered this vague, general statement as a charter for a church. If we are to accept the record of all four Gospels, Jesus was silent as to this directive in Mark, Luke and John. The passage is especially open to question because the Greek word for church, used here, is used only twice in the Gospels. There was no Aramaic word for church, and the original Christian groups were more in the nature of democratic communes than churches. Moreover the extra dignity and authority supposedly conferred on Peter is not consistent with the rest of the legend. In the very same passage in which Jesus was alleged to have made Peter the first pope, he rebuked him bitterly: "Get thee behind me, Satan: thou art a stumbling-block unto me; for thou mindest not the things of God but the things of men."

After a long and learned discussion of "The Origin of the Papacy" in his *Christianity, Past and Present*, Charles Guignebert, professor of the history of Christianity in the University of Paris, says: "That Christ had no intent to found the Catholic, Apostolic and Roman Church is a truth which it is no longer necessary to demonstrate. Consequently, there is no further need to prove that St. Peter did not consider himself pope and to show that it took a great deal of time—many centuries—for his successors to perceive that they might become popes. The Papacy is a creation of man, constructed little by little in the course of the Church's existence, by the logic of its development and by a series of historical accidents."

I shall not attempt to recapitulate here the long story of Christian mercies and Christian perversions which followed the initial manufacture of this new religion. Some popes preached and practiced love and service for the poor; others were murderers and grafters. It is doubtful if anything in all history can match the Crusades and the Inquisition in cruelty. All this is now far in the past even if it is not wholly forgotten.

But it is important to remember that the present primary gospel of Christian salvation is still a gospel of cruel vengeance. John 3:16, the most famous verse in the New Testament, says: "For God so loved the world, that he gave his only begotten Son, that whosoever believeth in him should not perish but have eternal life." It is not a gospel of freedom but of crime and punishment. It consigns the willful unbeliever to perish as a penalty even for honest disbelief. That doctrine is neither Catholic nor Protestant but Christian, and it does not belong in a free world.

3 Rescuing the "Poor Souls"

(Young Self—1917)

I pray every Sunday with my people. As we pray together for fellowship, peace, and faith, there comes upon me the joy of yearning with them for something beyond the pain of today. I feel that their hearts respond with mine in a great longing. When I have in my prayer much of tenderness and sympathy, I know that they are better satisfied with the morning's worship. But as I pray for ideals, I know that they are often begging for tomorrow's selfish victory. They believe that God will change the course of the universe to satisfy their wants. Because of my prayer they are failing to look reality in the face. I am a beggar leading beggars.

So I have stopped praying except when I must. I sit in my chair sometimes and try to think to God but I no longer try to find Him upon my knees. I seem to find more of God in the world when I am standing erect.

There is a tender mood that comes upon men when they think of the passing of their lives like a shadow. We have learned to call the mood reverence, and prayer has become its accepted form among nearly all races. It is the formal tribute of man to the Great Unknown that grips the destiny of us all. It is our common way of expressing the wonder of the Psalmist: "What is man that Thou art mindful of him?"

Even the most cynical of men cannot stifle the wonder that comes into his being when he considers the vastness and intricacy of life. We would be more than human if we did not partake of that wonder. And most of all when the great gift of life itself is about to be taken away and we come for the first time to see the value of our treasure, how our souls are prostrated in an agony of fearful hope! Gethsemane was not and is not a delusion.

But how much of prayer is a delusion and a useless superstition?

An old lady came to my house the other

day and, patting me on the shoulder, told me how much she hoped I would succeed in my new church. She promised to pray very earnestly that God would make the work fruitful. I thanked her in an embarrassed way and said good-bye. When she had gone I fell to thinking of the millions of useless prayers which have been offered up by lazy zealots as an excuse for real labor. I thought of the many times when prayer has been used by the chaplains of the rich to stifle the rebellion of the poor.

The case against prayer has been stated again and again by the men who have ceased to pray and by the men who have never prayed. I want to record here the sentiment of a man who still prays—with half a heart.

There are two attitudes the average preacher may take toward prayer. He may believe that prayer actually changes the course of the universe, or he may believe that prayer is simply a "good spiritual tonic" for a congregration which needs moral exercise.

When a man starts to examine the reality of prayer as a means of changing the course of external life he encounters the most painful chapter in the story of the intellectual degradation of the clergy. In an age of miracles and wonders when every real phenomenon was an inexplicable fact and no such thing as scientific analysis was known, prayer was recognized as the personal request of a favored subject to his Great Warrior or

Pet Chieftain. When the scientific awakening of the last century came, the natural conclusion of an intelligent preacher was that prayer had never proved its results and that as an institution of the church it should be examined with real scrutiny. But the attacks of scholarship were centered upon the Bible and outworn theology, so the preacher was permitted to do as he pleased with prayer. Since the foundations of Christianity were already trembling from the assaults of higher criticism, he let prayer alone. The result is that men who do not dare to believe in the Mosaic authorship of the Pentateuch still gather in great conventions and pray for the physical health of a missionary in China.

Now the proposition that the appendix of a certain missionary in China will become less inflamed if five thousand people in an American city ask God for his relief is one which is open to scientific analysis. If the parties in the case would submit to experiments the facts might be readily discovered. The doctors in China might arrange a clinic to take place simultaneously with the prayer-meetings in America and observe the effect of prayer-waves upon the afflicted missionary.

But, so far as I know, the members of a certain convention which met several years ago in a Western city and offered up prayers with me for the health of a missionary in China never inquired whether their prayers accomplished any physical result. They knew that their assumption of power to change physical facts was a lie.

They knew that the old promise, "Ask and it shall be given to you," as applied to most of the worthwhile things of life is a *lie*.

They would be unwilling to pay a postage stamp for a patent medicine which has failed to accomplish its promised results in as large a proportion of cases as prayer has, but they continue to class their credulity in the physical efficacy of prayer as "faith." They put this faith on a higher level than the gullibility of those rural audiences who spend hard-earned savings for tapeworm medicine sold by Demosthenic grafters. But I do not appreciate their distinction.

If prayer is to have recognition in the physical world, it must submit to physical tests. Three-cent gasoline, it was said, was recently invented by a Boston lawyer, but the automobile investors of the city did not pay any attention to the claim until it was scientifically experimented with. Then it was proved to be a failure.

Is the reconstruction of the universe by personal petition so unimportant an undertaking that no one need investigate it? Can the gigantic swindle of purgatorial and sick-get-better prayers which command so large a proportion of the money and loyalty of American Catholics and Protestants be passed over by the clergyman with a few words about "faith in the Unseen"?

The claim made by defenders of prayer as a

physical transformer is that prayer is on a "spiritual level" distinct from three-cent gasoline. Some prayer is. But the level of prayer is no higher than its aim, and when men spend time in interceding before God in the attempt to accomplish the results of medicine and muscle without resort to anything else, they must submit to comparison.

And comparisons are odious. They show that prayer as a physical transformer and restorer is more truly based upon superstition than any patent medicine on the market. Where prayer heals one, patent medicines heal five. The results must speak for themselves. Ten million prayers a day arise unanswered to God. During the war there were prayers for the soldiers of Europe by sympathetic Americans; there were prayers for the eternal conquest of the German arms by a million German mothers; there were prayers for the conquest of Russian, French, American, English, and Turkish murdering machines; there are prayer for a passing mark in examinations by schoolchildren; there are prayers for success in gambling on the stock market; there are endless prayers for rain, for dry weather and for salvation from lightning. . .

Why should we attempt to classify these prayers into "superstitious" and "intelligent"? In not a single case can it be proved that intercession before God affected His direction of the forces of war, lightning or plague. The dilemma of the old reasoners is unanswerable:

If God is an omnipotent and wise Father, then he does not need our personal pleadings to make Him realize the needs of mankind: If He is not such a Father, then the prayer is directed to an imaginary mind. If the universe is built upon the plan of conventional Christian theology, why pray at all?

The *failure* of prayer is a subject which is taboo among the clergy. We have learned to evade the real issue of the worthwhileness of a prayer for so long that we take ourselves seriously when we tell some afflicted sister who is about to lose her only son with tuberculosis: "If it is God's will, your prayers will be answered; never cease to pray." That is an evasive half lie. What we mean in our hearts is that the prayer will comfort the mother and do no harm to the son. The son will die if the physical laws of life make it inevitable.

I am saying these things at the risk of repeating very stale truths because I am repeatedly astonished by the number of people who still take intercessory prayer seriously. I meet sane, clearheaded businessmen, hard-working and cynical laboring men, who have failed to look the facts about prayer as a physical transformer squarely in the face. They would not allow a book agent to take up ten minutes of their time with a theory that has so little real evidence in its support as the theory of personal intercessory prayer. But they allow velvet-voiced preachers to prey upon their superstitions without a murmur.

The story of these velvet-voiced ones is uniform. We have not had our prayers answered because we have not known *how* to pray. (As if the Lord God our Father were not Himself responsible for the lisping intellect of His creatures.) We should learn to pray simply and trustfully. Men have always prayed to God our Father; therefore we should pray to Him as our Father. He may not always answer us according to our wishes, but out of the abundance of His wisdom He will do what is best for us. It may not seem best to us at the time, but if we will trust in Him, our way will be made clear. So we have in the prayer-meeting that optimism born of selfish desire which deliberately creates a universe contrary to all the facts of life because men are more interested in happiness than they are in truth. Men do not always want to *know*. They want something to believe. They have but a short time to live and a very small portion of that time to devote to the things of religion and ultimate destiny. The easy faith of the fathers with its magic priestcraft is offered to them. Faith, the preacher tells them, is beyond reason anyway. Why listen to the skeptic? Simple trust brings that peace of intellectual death which fills the collection box and enables men to go on with the more important tasks of earning a living.

But in spite of the faith of the prayer-meeting in the power of changing the universe by personal prayer, the great masses of men

are no longer able to believe in that kind of
prayer. They compromise by believing in
prayer as a means of making men more holy
and Christian. Prayer, they are willing to
believe, is a great spiritual tonic. Through
prayer, we come into communion with God,
even if He does not change the universe to
suit our desires.

Whether we can accept this belief depends
upon our hard-headedness. People might be
divided roughly into the hard-headed, the
mystical, and the soft-headed. I am among
the hard-headed. Not that I do not enjoy
poetry, a symphony orchestra or a spring
landscape. My critical reason is predominant
over my imagination and emotion to a
somewhat larger degree than among other
men. I have been converted twice in revival
meetings and have found profound emotional
experience in prayer, but the effectiveness of
those emotional crises was destroyed when I
calmly considered their meaning and value.
Never in my whole life have I been certain
that I have communed with anything higher
than my own emotional aspirations. When God
has met me on Sinai, He has always hidden
his face.

Now the soft-headed man labels his great
emotional moments "communion with God"
because the world tells him to. He has never
made any honest attempt to analyze his own
reactions and discover whether the assumption
of anything supernatural in his religious

experience is true. His mother has taught hi
at her knee to call the self-revelation of
childhood prayer communion with God.
Under the influence of that tradition and the
hypnotic power of a great revivalist he hears
the "call of God." It is a very real call from
the highest moral traditions and ideals of his
experience. He puts that experience into the
storehouse of his memory and perhaps gives
definite shape to it by adding the description
of some great religious leader. Now he has a
god to pray to. He believes in communion
through prayer.

The hard-headed man looks on at this
religious experience of the self-headed man
with lack of sympathy and sometimes
contempt. He does not understand it very well
But the mystic does. The mystic is a man of
imagination and insight who reaches the
conclusion that "the mystery of things" is
personal and that man can reach that Person
though direct communion. The mystic is not
an intellecutal infant, although he often
associates with such. Now I am a hard-headed
man, so I cannot discuss the mystic with any
fair appreciation, for I have striven hard after
the mystic's experience and have never been
able to find anything personal in religious
experience outside of the yearnings of my own
soul and the traditions of experience.

The painful truth about the position of the
mystic within the church is that his belief is
taken up by all sorts of undiscerning people
and applied to every imaginable superstition.

do not believe that one man in ten is able to comprehend the mystical point of view, but the preacher soon finds that it is a great advantage to define his own religious experience in these mystical terms. It sets him apart as a spiritual leader. So we often see the strange phenomenon of a congregation of hard-headed and anxiously selfish seekers after salvation creating their religious experience in the reflected light of their preacher's experience: and when the truth is known, the preacher is not a mystic but an imaginative, descriptive artist who has learned to paint his religious experience in colors his congregation can admire.

The responsibility for sham religious experience and false evaluation of prayer falls upon the clergy. They have thought loosely and spoken recklessly. They have defined the spoken recklessly. They have defined the aspirations of their hearts with a definiteness that the facts do not support. When they quietly analyze their experience in prayer, they are willing to admit that the voice of God which they heard in prayer may have been the voice of conscience and nothing else. For those few men who, when they have carefully and critically analyzed their own minds, feel the presence of God coming to them in prayer, I have nothing but envy. I would like to be one of them—but God has never blessed me with the sign.

What, then, is left of the reality of prayer? Prayer to me is nothing but a simple expression of human desire. There are times in our lives when we need to forget the small troubles and quarrels of the scramble we call life. Then it clears our vision for someone to express with us the higher hopes of universal service and brotherhood. That is why I still pray with my congregation for higher motives and ideals. I want to teach them through prayer something of higher aspiration.

And does not prayer have a real function as an expression of noble desire? Out of the darkness we have come and into it we will go. Everywhere is Death. The Mystery gives back no answer when we cry. The brave man looks into the darkness unafraid: He is terrified by no threat of the future but he would claim the Unknown for himself. He stretches out his hands to gain greater fullness of life. Priests and fear-mongers bring answers to his prayers. He scorns them for he is not asking for their answer. He is yearning for Life: He is on the great search which has no goal.

(Old Self—1974)

When I wrote down the above thoughts on prayer, I had never read the most famous article ever written on the subject, Sir Francis Galton's "Statistical Inquiries into the Efficacy of Prayer," published in *The Fortnightly Review*, August 1, 1872. I think that Galton, a famous scientist, was writing with tongue in cheek, but whether he was serious or satirical his article created a worldwide sensation in Christian circles. "The efficacy of prayer," he said, "seems to me as simple, as it is a perfectly appropriate and legitimate subject of scientific inquiry." Then he proceeded to note in statistical tables that the most prayed-over people in the world, the sovereigns of state and their royal associates, got sick and died at an earlier age than lawyers, doctors and military officers who enjoyed no such solicitude; that missionaries in foreign countries who were probably the beneficiaries of more fervent prayer than any other class of ordinary citizens seemed to die as readily as anybody else; and that "the distribution of stillbirths appears wholly unaffected by piety." He proposed that Christian prayer be tested by taking two sets of patients at a hospital who were suffering from some ailment like a fracture or an amputation, one set to be "markedly religious and piously befriended" and the other "remarkably cold-hearted and neglected." Then let the observers see if the experiment would "manifest a distinct proof of the efficacy of prayer." The challenge, of course, was never accepted.

Since Galton wrote his famous article, the belief in the efficacy of petitionary prayer has changed dramatically in Western society. Such prayer is now widely regarded as merely an emotional and ceremonial gesture having no effect on external events. The world moves on a more practical level. Although Jesus said: "Ask and it shall be given unto you," few people even bother to ask, and may skeptics echo the cynicism of Voltaire when he remarked: "What is the use of teasing God with prayers?" Voltaire's cynicism about prayer was echoed in the story told of a Swiss captain who prayed before a battle: "O God, if there is one, take pity on my soul if I have one."

The process of teasing God with selfish petitions would not be worth discussing if prayers were always personal and private. But public prayer has become an important instrument in social and religious propaganda. Priests and preachers do not observe the injunction of Jesus to pray in private, avoid advertising, and make the ceremony as simple as possible. The Protestant and Catholic forms of prayer compete with each other to the derogation of both, as anyone can testify who has listened to five over-long petitions to God during inaugural ceremonies for the President of the United States.

American etiquette in Christian prayer varies from the free-wheeling ad lib performances of Southern Baptists to the heavy, stylized Latin formulas of the Roman Catholic Church. The Southern Baptist divine stands straight up, closes his eyes while facing the congregation, and bleats out a long petitionary bellow of haths and doths in sixteenth century prose. He often begins each paragraph with an introductory assertion "Thou knowest, Lord", and then proceeds to catalogue for God all the most important events on the current moral landscape. Thus the public prayer becomes no so much a petition to God as an auxiliary sermon. The preacher imparts to God the necessary information and suggests what should be God's response. God usually obliges by implication and inference in the words of the preacher himslef.

Catholicism has been much more effective in developing prayer than Protestantism because the priest has been able to coordinate prayer into the Catholic system of rewards surrounding saints, indulgences and purgatory. Catholic saints do certain definite things for the faithful who pray to them, and this is far better than the guesswork answers to Protestant prayer. Anyone who has ever visited a Mexican Catholic church will appreciate the superiority of the Catholic technique. The walls of the church may be lined with pictures and paintings of Senor X and Senora Y who have been cured of a broken back or a consumptive lung by praying to Saint Z, and the back or lung may be included in the picture. This is much more satisfactory than answerless prayer.

Catholicism's greatest contrivance in the field of prayer has been purgatory. Although purgatorial ideas existed in Judaism, the Catholic doctrine of purgatory is a purely clerical invention having no authority in the New Testament or in the teachings of Jesus. The word is not even in the Bible. The Catholic concept was developed in the Middle Ages with the encouragement of several popes who based their purgatorial theories on the ancient practice of praying for the dead. Pope Innocent IV made purgatory official on March 6, 1254 when he sent a letter to the apostolic delegate in Greece describing an intermediate place between heaven and hell where there might be some fire but not all-consuming fire. "We," said Pope Innocent, "following the tradition and authority of the Holy Fathers, call that purgatory."

Purgatory was made even more official during the Council of Trent in 1564 when Pope Pius IV issued a bull prescribing for all Christians the belief that "there is a purgatory and that the souls detained there are helped by the prayers of the faithful." This last thought was an inspiration. Almost every human being feels some guilt about neglecting or mistreating deceased relatives and friends. Why should not the church develop a definite scheme for helping deceased friends up the ladder from purgatory to heaven through prayer? (Indulgences had already been developed to fit into this pattern.) The payments for such prayers were described as contributions, no fees. The profits, whatever they were called, were especially generous on All Saints Day.

When Innocent IV officially invented purgatory, he wisely suggested that it was a place for "small and slight sins," not for "grievous and capital sins." This guaranteed that there would always be a large purgatorial population since almost everybody has a number of small and slight sins to his discredit. This larger population meant more prayers and more revenue from guilt-ridden relatives.

The church wisely refused to guarantee a single reduced sentence for any soul in purgatory. As one Catholic authority on the subject has put it: "God does not make us partners in his knowledge....When we pray for souls in this world or in purgatory, we must not expect to know the results of our prayers, much less tell Him what ought to be results."

The Church was also wise in not documenting thoroughly the daily life of the souls in hell. That could be left to imagination and the poets. Dante probably knew more about the situation than any pope. He pictured sinners in purgatory as grouped along seven terraces that corresponded to the circles of hell, with an earthly paradise in a sphere on top of the finally redeemed souls. St. Francis de Sales hit upon the idea of describing all inhabitants of purgatory as both happy and agonized at the same time. "The sufferings of purgatory," he said, "are greater than any pains of this life, but the interior consolations enjoyed by the souls in purgatory are greater than any contentment which man can experience in this life." We shall say more about the pains and ecstasies of the after life in a later chapter.

Prayer is so tender and intimate a thing that

few people would ever think of it as a controversial political issue. But it became a bitter political issue in the United States in the 1960s because its devotees tried to force it into public classrooms in this country in spite of the established American policy of the separation of church and state. In Nassau County, New York, five parents of eleven children in public schools, a free thinker, two Jews, one Unitarian and one member of the Ethical Culture Society objected because their children every morning were made part of a brief religious exercise in which the children said in unison: "Almighty God, we acknowledge our dependence upon Thee, and we beg They blessings upon us, our parents, our teachers and our country."

The parents did not raise any strictly theological issue; their protest might just as well have come from Mohammedans or Roman Catholics—in fact their lawyer was a Roman Catholic. They raised a question of civil liberties under the First Amendment of the Constitution: "Congress shall make no law respecting an establishment of religion or prohibiting the free exercise thereof." This prayer, they alleged, innocuous as it seemed, helped to establish religion, and if any religion was to be established in the minds of their children they wanted to establish it themselves. They did not want any public tax-supported institution to undertake that responsibility.

Although their case was emotionally weak

because the prayer was deemed so innocuous, the five parents won a resounding victory. Even this simple prayer, said the Court, "reaches the constitutional wall of separation between church and state...the constitutional prohibition against laws respecting an establishment of religion must at least mean that in this country it is not part of the business of government to compose official prayers for any group of the American people to recite as part of a religious program carried on by government."

That was 1962. Later the same Court forbade the Lord's Prayer and Bible reading as parts of religious exercises in public schools for the same reasons. Yes, we have come a long way from the day when the Emperor Constantine made Christianity the state religion. Indignant and devout parents in several states have talked about a constitutional amendment permitting the re-entry of prayer into public classrooms, but they have been rudely surprised to discover that they received little support from the great established denominations in this country, Christian and Jewish. Most of America seems to be satisfied with the religious neutrality of our public institutions.

4 Dying and Lying

(Young Self - 1917)

I buried an old sea-captain the other day who
had been notorious for his capacity for
swearing. He had never belonged to a church
and never intended to belong to one. While
sailing into a quiet harbor one day he dropped
dead. His daughter wanted him buried by a
"liberal preacher," so the family sent for me.

I expected that the funeral would be a
distasteful affair; it is never pleasant to mix
syrup with vinegar. I could say nothing good

about the old man except that he had made a host of friends and that he had a good wife and daughter. Yet I knew that every word I said would be remembered by the family for months to come. They were hoping for the eulogy which should make their father's funeral like that of all respectable church elders. The words of praise had become almost as much a part of the funeral service as the flowers at the grave.

So I climbed into the cab which came for me just after lunch and spent my time on the long journey thinking of all the good things which may be said about human life at the funerals of profane sea-captains. If I were to speak the truth about this old sea-dog I would say something like this:

"My friends, I have come to you today to bury the remains of a friend who has passed out of this life. He was a good bluffer, a hearty liar, a careless father, and an indifferent citizen. I do not know where he is going. My only business here is to quiet as much as I can the grief of a wife and daughter who would not rest in peace without this silly bit of convention called a funeral.

"I am not going to make you cry because there is nothing to cry about. The man who died day before yesterday was quite old and decrepit. In another year he would have retired from the only work of which he was capable and become a burden upon his friends. It is much better to die in harness at the end of the race than to die of nursing in the stable. It is fortunate indeed that he died when he did.

"If I agreed with Jesus, I would say that the soul of this friend of yours is going straight to hell. But I do not agree with Jesus in several important particulars. I do not believe that the captain was any more responsible for his villainies than the good deacon, his father, who took him out of school at the age of fourteen and made him go to work with a crew of disreputable sailors. Angels could not have lived untainted in his environment. If the captain is going to hell for his vices, then a few hundred lawmakers and preachers should go with him.

"But I do not know whether there is a hell for the captain to go to. I am supposed to know all about hell and heaven, but then there are a good many things which I am supposed to know that I really do not know at all. For instance, I do not know whether the captain had a soul. Perhaps when he died, the thing called consciousness which seemed to have something to do with his brain died along with the body. Perhaps it is flying around in the air somewhere. It might be behind the jardiniere there in the corner.

"But do not be disturbed! If the captain's spirit is moving about us, it can have no great effect upon us. He cannot speak to us or touch us. The fact that he is alive in the room does not prove the truth of any of the superstitions from the New Testament which you would have me read. I am not at all sure that I want to live after the grave and, perhaps, if you knew what eternity holds for you, you would not want your friend to live either.

"Did you ever think of the terrors of eternal life? How flat and meaningless everything would be if we had a thousand years in which to perform it? The fact that we walk this way of life but once puts the stamp of importance upon all our deeds. If I had a thousand years to preach this sermon, how much interest would I have in it? It is only because in the midst of a short and crowded life, I have just twenty minutes of the 9th of March, 1917, to give this message to you that it has any significance to me. If you had all eternity to learn these facts, I would scarcely need to tell them to you.

"The dream of eternity is so popular with us because we are all like children reaching out for the moon. If we ever grasped the moon, we would be badly burned.

"The age of ghost stories has for the most part gone by, but the age of eternity day-dreams is still with us. We do not understand this thing we call death, and, standing on the great shore of the Unknown, we are overwhelmed by our own utter absence of knowledge. In that moment the priest comes to us and capitalizes on our fear. He wins us not because he satisfies our reason but because he has the only thing to which we can cling. While we are dumb with grief, the priest has words. His word-pictures of eternity, for a time at least, put our minds at peace.

"So I am here at a funeral today because society has not yet invented any celebration of the fact of death which is more appropriate than a funeral. I am supposed to mumble phrases about the blessed future when I do not know any more about that future than you do. I hope; you hope; we all HOPE. That is all any of us knows about hell, heaven, or eternity.

"It is a popular thing among priests of every religion to use the terrors of the Unknown Future to propagate some silly view of life. If I chose to follow in their way this afternoon I could make this fact of the death of your friend an occasion for a severe lecture in behalf of the dying Christian faith. I could warn you that only by belief in Jesus Christ and by loyalty to his church can you escape the terrors of everlasting torment. And you have become so accustomed to this spiritual bullying that you would not resent it. You are so lazy intellectually that you want me to solve the problem of death for you with theological gibberish. You do not want to think through the problem of death for yourselves because outside of your little house of cards is the Great Black Night of Fear.

"So I must tell you the obvious truth that Jesus Christ and all the other religious leaders of men have failed to solve the problem of death. Our friend the captain may be living and he may be dead. I am inclined to believe that he is living, but that is only a pet view of mine. It has no proof anywhere. Jesus said: 'In my Father's house are many mansions' but no man has ever returned from those mansions to give us a picture of their splendor. No man has ever risen from the dead and given us a real picture from beyond the grave. The New Testament has said that Jesus rose bodily from the grave, but there is no more proof for it than for the ascension of Mary Baker Eddy. The leaders of biblical criticism know this, but they are too 'scholarly' to apply common sense to the interpretations of the Bible. They admit that there is no adequate proof of the resurrection, but they save their souls (and salaries) by declining to say that there is any proof against its truth.

"The critics cannot say positively that Jesus Christ did not rise from the dead because no member of the American Historical Association was present at the grave to bear witness to that fact.

"And even if our friend the captain is now living with Jesus in immortality, I cannot guarantee his happiness in the spirit world. The 'reports' which have come to mankind through the mediums of spiritualism who seem to have access to that realm of spirit are dreary reading. After his blatant, cursing existence here on earth the captain would

scarcely be comfortable in any environment less
boisterous than a barroom.

"So I do not hold out any great hope for
your friend. He cannot logically be in the
heaven of Jesus Christ for he blasphemed him
from morning to night. He may have gone on
to a stage of higher consciousness which we as
yet cannot understand. He may be there in
the coffin.

"The only thing that we know about the
captain is that he has gone from us and that
we may never see him again.

"I am very glad that I have met you and I
hope that you will think seriously of the
problem of death as a result of this funeral."

But when I got to the house of the captain,
I looked into the face of the white-haired old
lady whose eyes were red with weeping. She
clung to my hand caressingly. "John was a bit
rough," she said, "but he was a good man.
Oh, I wish you could have met him. He was
the best husband in all the world. I don't
know what Nettie and I will do without
him."

And when Nettie came to meet me and we
were alone for a moment she whispered,
"Mother is all broken up by father's death—
she can hardly hold out through the funeral—
we were so glad that you were able to come

for the services. Mother's people were all Presbyterians, you know."

So, when the soloist had finished a wailing rendition of "Face to Face Shall I Behold Him," I arose and read the Scripture readings which every preacher knows. I read about the resurrection of Jesus and the raising of Lazarus. I read the dream of the Beautiful City. I read the decisive guarantees of immortality uttered by St. Paul. When I had finished I said:

"We are met here today to commemorate the passing over of another friend. He was a good friend and true and in the heart of every one of us there is an empty place which can never be filled. When we come to the Great Portal of Death and look back at our own lives, how much we find in them that might have been more perfect and more Christlike! And how keenly we appreciate the value of those simple virtues of love and friendship and kindliness!

"The friend whose death we commemorate today was not a king of any earthly kingdom; his passing over is not heralded by the grief of a nation. But he ruled over that kingdom which is more sacred than any broad domain; he ruled in the hearts of a fond wife and daughter and in the hearts of a host of loving friends. So he shall not go to his grave unhonored and unsung. We who have been his subjects in the little kingdom of love will speak over his grave the sorrows of the loss of a friend.

"Grief must always come to man when the life of some friend is suddenly taken away into the great Far Country. But the fact of death does not leave us without hope, for Jesus has told us: 'In my Father's house are many mansions; if it were not so I would have told you. I go to prepare a place for you.' In the sweetness of that promise we may find in death the joy of resurrection. Jesus tells us that beyond the Valley of the Shadow is the light of the Morning. Death shall not conquer the strong and kindly life of our friend.

"We who are left in the little circle of friends will some day hear the last summons. Let us live in the way of the Master that we shall go to meet our friend with joy. Let us keep the broken circle full of love and helpfulness until it is united Over There...."

When the soloist had sung "Nearer My God to Thee," and I was about to go, the little old lady met me at the door. There were tears streaming down her cheeks but her face was radiant.

"Thank you so much for coming," she said. "You spoke so beautifully. I wish John could have heard you. Perhaps he did." "Yes, I hope he did," I said. "I am very glad that I was able to help you."

And so as I rumbled back home in the cab over a rough cobblestone road, I thought again of the age-old truth that the human heart is mightier than the love of truth. I had always believed that the truthseeker must choose between human life as it is and human life as it ought to be. He who loves men supremely must seem to slay happiness in order that truth shall come. So I had always thought. But in the moment of testing all these "principles" had gone from me. I had looked into an old woman's tear-stained face— and I had lied, jubilantly and freely. I was overwhelmingly glad that I had! Whereupon I had more patience with G. K. Chesterton and Cardinal Newman.

And I fell to thinking of the parable of the great supper and the men who made excuses for tending to their wives, lands and oxen instead of going to the feast. I had never before realized that it might be that the wives, lands and oxen were more important than the feast. There are times when it may seem more important to save a woman's heart than to win a whole city to truth. Jesus said that everyone who followed him must sacrifice home and family. But what of the family? So I asked with the truthseeker: What of love and friends? Shall I tell the truth and break a woman's heart?

I lied. I lied because the truth we can tell about death is so trivial and unimportant that it is scarcely worth any woman's heart. Funerals are not built for truth anyway. They are built for comfort. There will come a time, no doubt, when man will be brave enough and wise enough to look deep into the heart of the great mystery. But the truth about death will never come through funerals. It will come when men have become so brave and honest

Some of My Best Friends Are Christians

that they are willing to go to their graves
without funerals. It will come when preachers
no longer have to break hearts to tell the truth.

(Old Self—1974)

That Blanshard of 1917 was certainly a
sentimental young liar in a funeral crisis, and
I hereby repudiate him.That Young Self, of
course, was subject to the double pressure of
his fellow human beings and the institutional
traditions of his calling. He could not be
completely truthful about death and
immortality and remain in a Christian pulpit.

I am afraid that that generalization applies
to almost all Christian clergymen even today.
They are expected to lie a little over the
caskets of their people. They are compulsive
institutional liars in the area of death even
when they are honest in regard to almost
every other aspect of the faith.

Assuming that I can now be reasonably
honest about death, I will be reasonably polite
also, and not imitate H. L. Mencken who once
brushed off the clergy by saying: "What is the
function that a clergyman performs in the
world? Answer: He gets his living by assuring
idiots that he can save them from an
imaginary hell. It is a business almost
indistinguishable from that of a seller of snake
oil for rheumatism."

Historically, life after death has been a great
field for human imagination. Many literary

artists have worked this field and emerged as imaginative geographers of heaven, hell, purgatory and the Last Judgment. To explore their explorations is an adventure in itself.

The Christian heavens and hells are not quite as interesting or varied as those of other religions. *The Hastings Encyclopedia of Religion and Ethics* gives us a very good sketch of Buddhist and Muslim hells and heavens. The Buddhist and Muslim heavens are far more interesting than our dreary, sexless assemblies of psalm singers and harp players. Christian hells are more interesting than Christian heavens but they cannot match the hells of other faiths.

The dead Buddhist who is destined for heaven may have successive mutations after death, becoming a god, an animal or a bird. No Christian has such a fascinating choice. If a Buddhist is consigned to one of eight hells in the Buddhist system, his fate is never monotonous. In Hell Number 2 he is cut up into eight or sixteen pieces; in Hell Number 6 he is fixed on spikes and burnt alive. If he is not consigned to one of the eight major hells, he may be sent to one of the 136 minor ones. In the hell of dung he is pierced by worms. In the hell of hot ashes he is smothered. Buddhism also provides eight ice hells where the frozen flesh of the victims "exfoliates in the form of flowers." The lowest Buddhist hell is 1,800 leagues in diameter, 5,400 in circumference and at least 20,000 leagues down. No geography of Christian hells has ever been so complete.

Muslim hells, as described in the Koran, are also ingenious. The fire is seventy times as hot as fire on earth and Allah makes the bodies of all suffering infidels larger than other bodies so that they can suffer more. The victims are bitten by serpents as large as two hundred camels and by scorpions as large as mules. The bites create pain for forty years.

To balance these orgies of pain, the Muslim heaven is made lush and sexy. Its walls are of gold and silver bricks with musk for mortar. Its "large-eyed damsels of modest glance" serve the men in many ways. The Muslim saints "recline on couches on green cushions" and are waited on by "eternal youths with goblets, ewers and a cup of flowing wine. No headache shall they feel therefrom, nor shall their wits be dimmed."

No Mussulman in paradise ever needs to sleep at all, and night and day he is given the powers of a hundred males to have connections with many women. The rights and privileges of the women are not so clearly prescribed. It is not surprising that Isak Dinesen, in speaking of the contrast between Christian and Muslim heavens, mentioned the "erotic aloofness of the founder of Christianity which has left his disciples in a kind of void" whereas Mohammedanism gives its men "the formidable, indomitable potency of the Prophet."

When Jesus began to preach, it was soon evident that he believed in some kind of life after death. He frequently referred to heaven and hell. His chief emphasis, however, was not on heaven and hell as such but on his own Second Coming in what the scholars call the parousia. Paul echoed this vision in I Thessalonians 4:13-18 with a definite order of precedence for the Last Judgment. "For the Lord himself shall descend from heaven with a shout, with the voice of the archangel and with the trump of God; and the dead in Christ shall rise first; then we that are alive, that are left, shall together with them be caught up into the clouds, to meet the Lord in the air: and so shall we ever be with the Lord."

There is no doubt that Jesus preached a hell of real fire, along with a heaven for believers. Here are some of passages which record Jesus' interpretation of hell:

Mark 3:29. "Whosoever shall blaspheme against the Holy Spirit hath never forgiveness, but is guilty of an eternal sin."

Mark 9:43 ". . . if thy hand cause thee to stumble, cut it off; it is good for thee to enter into life maimed, rather than having thy two hands to go into hell, into the unquenchable fire."

Matthew 5:22 ". . . whosoever shall say Thou fool, shall be in danger of the hell of fire.

Matthew 10:14 "And whosoever shall not rece

you, nor hear your words, as ye go forth out of that house or that city, shake off the dust of your feet. Verily I say until you, it shall be more tolerable for the land of Sodom and Gomorrah in the day of Judgment than for that city."

Matthew 13:40 ". . . so shall it be in the end of the world. The Son of Man shall send forth his angels, and they shall gather out of his kingdom all things that cause stumbling, and them that do iniquity, and shall cast them into the furnace of fire."

Matthew 13:49 "So shall it be at the end of the world: the angels shall come forth, and sever the wicked from among the righteous and shall cast them into the furnace of fire: there shall be the weeping and the gnashing of teeth."

Matthew 23:33 ". . . ye serpents, ye offspring of vipers, how shall ye escape the damnation of hell?"

Matthew 25:41 "Then shall he say also unto them on the left hand, Depart from me, ye cursed, into the eternal fire which is prepared for the devil and his angels."

Jesus left a great many questions about heaven and hell unanswered. If the Judgment Day should come so quickly, what of the fate of those who never had the opportunity to hear the Christian message? If, as the creeds say, there is resurrection of the body for believers, which bodies will be revived, old or new? What about mixed particles of bodies whose ashes have been commingled with the bodies of other deceased?

The most controversial questions about the Christian heaven have usually centered on sex. The Sadducees in Mathew 22:23-30 tried to trap Jesus into a contradiction or a dilemma by posing the question: Which wife would a man choose in paradise if he had been married seven times and all seven of his wives had pre-deceased him? Jesus replied that "in the resurrection they neither marry nor are given in marriage." The apparent assumption was that in heaven sexual desire would taper off.

This answer has not always been considered definite enough. Some Catholic exegetes have given more definite replies. Father Robert E. Kekeisen who operated for many years the "Ask and Learn" column in America's leading Catholic weekly has filled in more definite answers. "Man will have a glorified or spiritualized body ... subtlety or the power of passing through material objects ... all the humors and even the hair and nails. Neither will there be any use of sex by the resurrected body. The reason for this is that the number of the elect, or saints, will be completed at the end of the world, and consequently there will be no need of reproduction."

Father Kekeisen conformed to the standard

Catholic thesis that the purpose of sex is not pleasure but children, and presumably heaven did not need any more children. He did not take up the question as to which teeth would be resurrected with the body or, in fact, whether there would be any teeth. Tertullian had preceded him in his analysis and had said that there would be teeth in resurrected bodies but not for chewing. Presumably they would be for smiling.

Through the centuries Christianity has been much more efficient in describing hell than in describing heaven. The Christian heaven is colorless and musically incomplete although it is overrun with a multitude of winged angels who keep repeating hosannas industriously to the sound of a harp. The Christian hell, on the other hand, is a varied and stimulating place. Many great priests and preachers of Catholicism and Protestantism have elaborated upon its features. Even Mark Twain noted some of these values when he said: "Heaven for climate; hell for society."

Two famous Catholic specialists in hell were St. Thomas Aquinas and Ignatius Loyola. Loyola, founder of the Jesuits, told Christians how to think about hell in his *Spiritual Exercises:* "This is a meditation on hell ... To see in imagination the great fires, and the souls enveloped, as it were, in bodies of fire. To hear the wailing, the screaming, cries and blasphemies against Christ our Lord and all His saints. To smell the smoke, the brimstone, the corruption and rottenness. To taste bitter things, as tears, sadness, and remorse of conscience. With the sense of touch to feel how the flames surround and burn souls."

Aquinas who believed that "few" were saved from hell and that "very many" were damned, invented the idea of a balcony in heaven from which the blessed would be given "a perfect sight of the punishment of the damned." Thus a Christian man could look down from heaven at the suffering of his heretical wife and rejoice in her agony as the logical punishment for her sin.

The Church has not neglected the education of children in this field. In the middle of the nineteenth century a certain Father J. Furniss C.S.S.R. wrote a book for children called *The Sight of Hell* which sold more than four million copies. It contained this vivid description of how a sinful girl will be treated in hell: "See! On the middle of that red hot floor stands a girl. She looks about sixteen years old. Her feet are bare. She has neither shoes nor stockings. . . . Listen, she speaks. "I have been standing with my bare feet on this red hot floor for years. . . . Look at my burnt and bleeding feet. Day and night my only standing place has been this red hot floor. . . . Let me go off this burning floor for one moment, only for one single short moment.'

"Look into this little prison. In the middle

of it there is a boy. . . . His eyes are burning like two burning coals. Two long flames come out of his ears. . . . There is a sound like a kettle boiling. . . . Hear what it is. The blood is boiling in the scalded veins of that boy. The brain is boiling and bubbling in his head. . . . The little child is in this red hot oven. Hear how it screams to come out. See how it turns and twists itself about in the fire. It beats its head against the roof of the oven. . . . "

Although I have cited these Catholic selections about hell, no one should think that Catholic hells are any worse than Protestant hells. Luther and Calvin could match any pope in the fervor of their brimstone gospels. Calvinistic Jonathan Edwards, the famous preacher of colonial New England, rivaled St. Thomas Aquinas as a delineator of hell. He seemed to gloat with special relish over "sinners in the hands of an angry god." The two greatest American Protestant evangelists of this century, Billy Sunday and Billy Graham, may both be rated as specialists in hell, skillful exploiters of the fear of death.

Billy Graham has also become a specialist in the Second Coming, bravely predicting that Christ will come in the very near future. In 1965 during a moment of great tension in the Arab-Israel dispute he was asked what his solution of the conflict might be. He replied that the matter would soon be settled by Christ's Second Coming.

Billy Graham is one of a large company of

Christian leaders who, through the ages of Christian history, have predicted the Second Coming, citing specific verses in the New Testament. Some believers have relied so heavily on these verses that they have sold all their worldly goods and waited on mountain tops for the arrival of the Lord. Gibbon and Voltaire both described a great movement of such believers in the tenth century when certain verses in Revelation were used as a definite warning of the end of the world. The end was also predicted in the period of the Great Plague (1345-1350); and in the eighteenth century one prophet set the actual date for October 13, 1736. In 1806 the people of Leeds were terrorized when a hen began to lay eggs marked "Christ is coming." There was no local SPCA to punish the culprits who had inked the eggs and forced them back into the hen's body for a new kind of second coming.

One thing that has deflated the Second-Coming Christians is the time schedule of modern astronomy with its billions of light years. A world which began in 4004 B.C. cannot be reconciled with quasars. The word "quasar" dates from 1964 and refers to quasar-stellar sources of energy. The astronomers now tell us that many parts of the universe appear to be several billion light years away and that of 150 quasars uncovered during the 1960s two are estimated to be nine billion light years distant. One, we are informed, may be 500 billion miles in diameter, and it may be brighter than all the stars of the Milky Way combined. The predictions about the future are equally non-biblical. In 1973 an eminent scientist, speaking in honor of the five hundredth anniversary of the birth of Copernicus, declared that the ultimate collapse of the universe into a single "black hole" seemed inevitable. The only hopeful element in his prophecy was that the end might be forty billion years ways.

When we face such a schedule on the way to the Great Oblivion, probably the best thing to do is to retreat to poetry:

Ah, make the most of what we yet may spend,
Before we too into the Dust descend;
Dust unto Dust, and under Dust to lie,
Sans Wine, sans Song, sans Singer, and —
    sans End!

5 Christianity and Sex

(Old Self - 1974)

In approaching the subject of Christianity and sex I must confess at the outset that I do not have an open or charitable mind on the subject. Christianity officially stands for love and honor between the sexes, for faithfulness to the marriage bond and security for children in the Christian home. No one can deny that it has done much to preserve the monogamous family. If it has failed to regulate successfully so explosive a faculty as human sex, it cannot

---

alone be held accountable for such failure.

But it has gone far beyond negative failure and become a major obstacle to successful sexual life. Its sexual code has been controlled and distorted for centuries by clerical antisexual extremists who have ignored the fact that man's most natural resource for attaining joy is sex.

Today's Christian outlook on sex is more lenient than Victorian Puritanism or Pauline aversion but it is still so far from complete realism that it constitutes a very serious obstruction to sane living. And it should be noted that it is Christianity itself, not its step-parent Judaism, which is the chief offender. The Yahweh of the Old Testament was savage and anti-female in imposing his sexual code upon his people but he never approached the foolish negativism of Paul, Augustine, Thomas Aquinas and—yes, of Jesus himself.

The primary defect of the New Testament in the area of sex is ambiguous and other-worldly escapism. The Christian pioneers were obviously afraid of sex. The Old Testament leaders, although they were offensively pornographic at times, did have the merit of talking about sex frankly. They discussed rape, incest, sodomy and prostitution with gutsy candor. The Christianity of the New Testament is priggish and evasive in comparison.

In discussing Christianity and sex I shall exercise an author's license and depart from the framework I have used in previous chapters, plunging directly into a discussion of the present situation without stopping to discuss my views in 1917. The world has moved so far and so fast in sexual matters since 1917 that my youthful views on the subject do not now seem worth recording.

The Christian attitude toward sex is due partly to entrenched and dogmatic attitudes toward women. The temple of Christianity is a male temple. God is male, Jesus is male, popes are male, and until recently all Protestant clergymen have been male. At the great Vatican Council of 1962-65, in an institution where male priests were far outnumbered by female nuns, the celibate male masters did not have a single female delegate at the opening sessions, and later female representation was only nominal.

This Christian anti-female syndrome goes back to the beginning. In the Garden of Eden Adam was first created by God—a male—as a solitary resident, and Eve was later manufactured out of his rib as a divine afterthought. In the Garden the Fall of Adam was the great tragedy. Presumably woman was already so low that she did not have so far to fall. She yielded to the serpent and then tempted the man to eat of the forbidden fruit. Some theologians delicately insist that the forbidden fruit was not copulation. It was "concupiscence"—which is broader than copulation. But Mark Twain knew better. He said it was copulation, and most of the world has agreed with Mark Twain.

So the male authors of the Bible began as male chauvinists by blaming the woman, and they later qualified as hypocrites by classifying man's greatest delight as Original Sin. Since a naked woman acted as the temptress in the affair, she was naturally blamed as chief offender. The man yielded to her wiles. The devil approached the man through her.

After Jesus came, the anti-female syndrome of the Old Testament was strengthened immeasurably by that twisted little man, St. Paul. Paul laid down appalling rules for female subjection in Christian life. Apparently the notion of the equality of the sexes had never occurred to him. His Christian God had decreed subordination of the woman in every aspect of life. The man was the head of the woman as Christ was the head of the Church. The wife must obey the husband as her overlord. Her Christianity came to her through him. "But I would have you know that the head of every man is Christ, and the head of the woman is the man" (I Cor. 11:3). "...the man is not of the woman, but the woman of the man." "I suffer not a woman to teach" (I Tim. 2:12). "It is shameful for a woman to speak the Church" (I Cor. 14:35).

Paul capped his antisexual philosophy with the expression of the opinion that a man should refrain from intercourse with all females if possible. ("It is good for a man not to touch a woman.") Later he did concede that it was better to marry than to burn, and in I Cor. 7, he made his concession to sex in marriage reluctantly but quite specifically. "Let each man have his own wife, and let each woman have her own husband. Let the husband render unto the wife her due; and likewise also the wife unto the husband. The wife hath not power over her own body, but the husband; and likewise also the husband hath not power over his own body, but the wife. Defraud ye not one of the other, except it be by consent for a season, that ye may give yourselves unto prayer, and may be together again, that Satan tempt you not because of your incontinency. But this I say by way of concession, not of commandment. Yet I would that all men were even as I myself." Presumably he was celibate and took glory in that condition, but his rules for marriage would, in the absence of contraception, populate the earth with an oversupply of Christians. In fact, his rules for rendering "her due" and "his due" support the Catholic notion of large families.

After St. Paul, the other great antisexual pioneer of the early Church was St. Augustine. Unlike Paul, Augustine had lived a wild and indulgent sexual life in his youth, having one mistress who was his constant companion for nine years. This lady, who bore a child of his, was finally brushed off without marriage and the young Augustine acquired another mistress. There must have been something revolting in his personal sex life since he turned against all women and all sexual joy in later life. He did not go as far in renunciation as his predecessor Origen, who castrated himself to restrain his sinful impulses, but apparently he came very close to that solution.

The whole apparatus of medieval monasticism probably owes more to the neuroses of Augustine than to Church law itself. He it was who hit upon the idea that sexual intercourse was permissible only for procreation. The New Testament itself, in spite of Catholic exegetes, does not support this notion. Augustine was also partly responsible for the Christian tradition of shame concerning the genitals, particularly concerning the erect penis. In describing the experience of Adam and Eve he said: "The first human pair, on experiencing in the flesh that motion which was indecent because disobedient, and on feeling the shame of their nakedness, covered their offending members with fig leaves."

Thomas Aquinas, although he came eight centuries after Augustine, copied the Augustinian dogmas on sex and became the Church's third great expert on the subject. In his *Summa* Aquinas contended that "man is the beginning and end of woman" and that virginity "unseared by the heat of sexual desire" is superior to marriage. "A woman's sole purpose in marrying," he proclaimed, "should be motherhood." So he became the celibate father of the modern anti-birth-control movement. Aquinas and his followers condemned that sexual pleasure which accompanies copulation. Two popes who came after Aquinas, Clement VIII and Paul V, declared that anybody should be denounced to the Inquisitor of the Faith who declared that kissing, touching and embracing for the sake of sexual pleasure were not grievous sins. With this background in view, we come to the two great areas of sexual life in which Christianity has distorted reality by promulgating half-truths and outright distortions of physiological fact. Let us describe them in order.

Birth Control and Abortion

Birth control is by far the most important area of conflict between Christianity and normal sexual life. Over-population threatens a large part of the world with disasters almost as complete as those of nuclear war. The world is said to be adding about 125 persons every minute to its totals, more than one million a week. The earth, with fewer than four billion today, may reach ten billion within fifty years. At present, with tremendous food shortages in many countries, more than two-thirds of the world's population is undernourished. What will be the state of affairs when we reach ten billion? One answer is: Look at India.

Christian opposition to birth control is usually thought of as an exclusively Catholic phenomenon because the hierarchy of the Roman Catholic Church has taken the lead in fighting contraception while most non-Catholic Christians have swung over to its support. In the United States, however, it was puritanical Protestant opposition rather than Catholic conservatism which gave the nation its first anti-birth-control legislation. Anthony Comstock, a conservative Protestant, produced the first public pressure that induced Congress to pass the first anti-birth-control law.

The law was a strange mixture of confusion and evasion. It attacked obscenity and lasciviousness without definitely prohibiting contraception. It banned the use of the mails for any lewd and lascivious literature without telling the world what lewd and lascivious literature was. At that time birth control was a "naughty" subject, too shameful to be talked about frankly in good society. The vulcanization of rubber had been discovered in the 1840s, but the average husband or wife did not yet know what a condom or pessary was. (The Comstock law was passed in 1873.) It took about sixty-three years after the passage of the general law before the federal courts in 1936 finally ruled that contraception was not obscene per se. Cardinal Hayes did not like this, since the mails were soon flooded with real information on the subject, and some of his own people laughed when he said that "little children came trooping down from heaven."

Today the Catholic Church, because its power structure is still a celibate dictatorship, is able to keep its extreme anti-birth-control prohibition intact, but the better educated Catholic people have long since deserted their hierarchy on the issue. Every responsible poll of American Catholic and non-Catholic opinion in recent years has confirmed the fact that Catholic women are as ready to champion and use contraceptives as the women of other faiths. Birth control is now an accepted American welfare measure, with federal and state funds supporting the birth-control movement openly.

The outcome has been the result of a long and bitter struggle against clerical power. Two predominantly Catholic states, Massachusetts and Connecticut, were the last states to permit birth-control clinics. They yielded finally only in 1965 when the Supreme Court handed down a decision establishing the "right of privacy" for the marriage bed. Long before this, women of wealth and influence had joined the redoubtable Margaret Sanger in her battle to make family planning a basic civil right in our society.

The birth-control battle has been a revealing struggle, and also a rather frightening struggle. On the Catholic side the propaganda has been based on carefully manufactured scriptural fraud. August theologians have waved copies of the Bible and of the Church Fathers and at the same time have distorted both the biological and historical facts. In many local political circles this clerical pressure has been translated into political pressure.

One reason for the fraudulent propaganda on birth control is that the Catholic Church, in spite of Augustine and Thomas Aquinas, waited a long time to make its stand against contraception official. Its Canon Law was issued in 1917 without a clear prohibition on the subject. Then in 1930 Pope Pius XI, after long cogitation and much adverse advice—it was said that about half his cardinals wanted a permissive statement on birth control—finally issued in his encyclical on Christian Marriage the ukase which banned all contraception except the rhythm method. Said Pius, with a magisterial flourish: "The Catholic Church, to whom God has entrusted the defense of the integrity and purity of morals, standing erect in the midst of the moral ruin which surrounds her, in order that she may preserve the chastity of the nuptial union from being defiled by this foul stain, raises her voice in token of divine ambassadorship and through Our mouth proclaims anew: Any use whatsoever of matrimony exercised in such a way that the act is deliberately frustrated in its natural power to generate life is an offense against the law of God and of nature, and those who indulge in such are branded with the guilt of grave sin."

Pius XI could not find any good quotation

in scripture to back up this sweeping claim—
Jesus never said anything on the subject—so
he fell back on the old story of Onan and
Tamar in the 38th chapter of Genesis and
pretended that it constituted divine authority
for the restrictive Catholic view. Not until the
Second Vatican Council was this ancient and
obscene story rejected by Catholic theologians
as a mandate against contraception. As the
Jewish Encyclopedia has made clear, the Onan
story was never intended to be a parable
against birth control but a warning to Jews
that they should obey the Jewish law of
inheritance.

Onan's brother in the story had died and,
according to Jewish tradition, Onan had the
unpleasant duty of taking his deceased
brother's widow Tamar unto wife, although he
did not fancy her and did not want to have a
child by her. So he "went in to her," spilled
his seed on the ground, and emerged from
the tent only to be promptly slain by the
Lord. Then Tamar, bent on getting revenge in
the form of a son from somebody, dressed
herself up as a prostitute, waylaid her own
father-in-law and attained her goal. It is
perfectly clear from the summary of the
Jewish law of inheritance in Deuteronomy 25:
7-10 that *coitus interruptus* was not the basic sin
for which Onan was punished. It was his
refusal to give his brother an heir.

At the Second Vatican Council of 1962-65
there were many rumblings of dissatisfaction

over the antiquated Catholic rule on birth control, but Pope Paul VI stood firm against reform, after blocking open discussion in the main sessions and rejecting the views of the majority of his own commission on the subject. He made reform virtually impossible as long as he is pope by issuing in 1968 his encyclical *Humanae Vitae*, the most antiscientific Christian pronouncement of the century. The mere issuance of such a ukase by a religious leader might not be considered a very serious obstacle to the on-rushing world movement for birth control, but the Vatican as a political institution still has enough power to sabotage world cooperation in many ways. This is particularly true in such Catholic countries as those of Latin America. Pope Paul followed up his extremist encyclical of 1968 in 1970 with a fifteen-page instruction to all papal nuncios and apostolic delegates to fight every government-supported contraceptive program throughout the world.

Even in the United States, where a majority of working priests probably favor the right of birth control, the bishops of the American church voted 143 to 20 in 1969 to protest "the ever-expanding role, both at home and abroad, of the government in the matter of population control through limitation of births." (The bishops, of course, are appointed and promoted by the pope.) In March 1971, the official spokesman on family life for the United States Catholic Conference protested that it was improper for the government to issue a postage stamp bearing a chaste picture of a man, a woman and two children, with the inscription, "Family Planning."

Strictly speaking, the right of abortion should not be considered a religious issue but an issue of civil rights for women. It has become an important church-state issue because the Catholic Church has chosen to make it such. When the Supreme Court declared in January 1973, that the "right of privacy . . . is broad enough to encompass a woman's decision whether or not to terminate her pregnancy," American law challenged Catholic law eyeball to eyeball. The Court's decision was a victory for the theory that a woman has a right to control her own body, and it was at the same time the most direct and complete defeat for Catholic dogma in our history.

The American Catholic hierarchy struck back with fury. The Court, said Cardinal Patrick O'Boyle of Washington, has committed a "hideous and heinous crime." Our American law, said the National Conference of Catholic Bishops, implies a "recognition of the law of God . . . and must conform to it . . . we reject the opinion of the United States Supreme Court as erroneous, unjust and immoral." From that point forward the issue of abortion became, partially at least, a test of competitive power between secular and religious institutions.

No one, of course, can deny that abortion presents a far more difficult moral choice than birth control. It is not harmless and it involves psychological as well as physical risks. It raises serious moral questions concerning the slender dividing line between health and homicide. It can be justified only by examining all aspects of the problem. The significant aspects include the sacrifice of millions of lives of pregnant women who have sought out abortion mills and unskilled surgeons under the old laws, the great improvement of modern medical techniques under which abortion has become relatively easy and cheap, the economic responsibilities of modern women which make the unwanted child more than ever unwanted, the shattered health of many pregnant women who cannot stand the additional strain of additional children. Most important of all, women have independent civil rights in a sane society, and theirs should be the choice whether to terminate a pregnancy or take the risks of abortion.

The American Civil Liberties Union, a pioneer in this field, puts the emphasis upon every woman's right as a woman. It holds, "that every woman, as a matter of her right to the enjoyment of life, liberty and privacy, should be free to determine whether and when to bear children. It is not a matter for the state to control." And the Union added that laws prohibiting abortion also promote unjustified inequality between classes in our society because "the rich can violate the law with impunity, but the poor are at the law's mercy."

This last point seems to have been almost ignored by the Catholic hierarchy. Its arguments have centered about an abstract entity called "life" which, upon examination, turns out to be the so-called life of the fetus, not the life of the mother. In fact, the old Catholic rule of the equality of mother and fetus in childbirth—the one cannot be saved at the expense of the other—is still on the Catholic books and still technically binding on Catholic hospitals and doctors.

Margaret Sanger—I knew her well—originally became interested in the problem of abortion when she saw long lines of poorly clad women in New York's East Side, standing on the sidewalk waiting to secure $5 abortions from illegal abortion mills. That vignette of agony should be supplemented by the statistic that at least one million illegal abortions were performed in the United States each year in the years before the operation was legalized. If so many women wanted abortion so much that they were willing to accept the risks of the old system, it is foolish to assert that reversion to the old system will stop them in the future.

The Supreme Court essentially agreed with the ACLU in its 1973 decision. It brushed aside the Catholic claim that life as defined by the law begins at conception, and it ruled that a fetus, particularly in the early stages of pregnancy, is not a whole person. It neatly divided the period of pregnancy into three sections or trimesters and it legalized virtually all abortions during the first two trimesters, with the advice of a physician. It even made abortion permissible during the last three months "where it is necessary, in appropriate medical judgment, for the preservation of the life or heath of the mother."

Perhaps one reason for the fury of the Catholic hierarchy over the Court's decision was that in the debate of the issues its theologians were caught with their citations down. They had pretended that their extreme reasoning in classifying all abortion as murder had the sanction of Christian scripture and the support of Church history. The claim was not justified, and the Court provided fruitful and scholarly footnotes to prove it. Jesus never said anything against abortion, and the Catholic Church for many centuries sanctioned some rights of abortion. St. Augustine had produced a calendar of unborn fetal life which provided a "soul" for male fetuses at forty days, and for female fetuses at eighty days, and his fantastic antiscience was generally accepted by Catholic theologians for centuries. Even Aquinas accepted abortion as justified during the early months of pregnancy. The present, extreme anti-murder dictum of the Catholic hierarchy on abortion did not jell until the nineteenth century.

Thus far in the abortion battle in the United States the overwhelming majority of Protestants and Jews seems to be willing to leave the decision about abortion to the woman and her physician. But Catholic canon law on the subject remains unchanged, making no moral distinction between ordinary abortion and therapeutic abortion, the kind required to save the life of a mother. Canon 2350 remains unmodified even by the Second Vatican Council. It still reads: "Those who procure abortion, not excepting the mother, incur, if the effect is produced, an excommunication *latae sententiae* reserved to the Ordinary [bishop]; and if they be clerics they are moreover to be deposed."

The Catholic-dominated Right to Life Committees which led the struggle against abortion in the United States in the 1960s and 1970s fought strenuously against any attack on the "innocent fetus." It is interesting to note that according to the time-honored theology of their Church the fetus is not innocent and has not been innocent since the Fall of Man. Under the doctrine of Original Sin, God himself enters into every womb and conditionally damns the fetal soul unless and until it can be redeemed by Christian salvation. O consistency! thy name is not Christian theology.

The Supreme Court, we hope, settled the moral as well as the legal issue by ruling that a nonviable (incapable of life) fetus is not to be considered a "whole person" either under common law or under our present Fourteenth Amendment. Although this is sound reasoning, we do not think that the ordinary man will be moved by such abstractions. He will be more likely to ask: What will happen to my wife if she gets pregnant unwittingly? Must we have unwanted children in our home? Shouldn't my wife be the one to answer these questions in the way she chooses? Some Catholic men may even ask the disrespectful question: What right does a celibate bishop who has never been pregnant have to answer these questions for my wife?"

Marriage and Divorce

That strange union of flesh and spirit called marriage has been exploited to the limit by the Christian clergy for many centuries until many misguided citizens have come to accept the notion that the institution itself is a Christian invention. Those devout citizens should read their history. Although no one questions their high moral aims, priests and preachers of all faiths have arrived on the marital scene as comparatively recent mendicants, possessing no moral sanction higher than their own professional interests. Even under present American law, since ours is a secular state, the preacher, priest or rabbi is present at a marriage ceremony only by legislative courtesy.

The "real" marriage is created by secular law. The divine who participates gets his authority from the state, not the other way around.

At the present time marriage and divorce as controversial Christian issues are largely Catholic issues. Protestants, in general, take a very broad view of marriage and divorce as well as mixed marriage. They do not claim exclusive rights over the marriage of their members and they accept the right of divorce. If a Protestant marries a Catholic before a Catholic priest, his Protestant church grants full recognition to the validity of the Catholic ceremony. Protestants who marry Catholics in a Protestant ceremony are not required to sign any pledge to rear their children as Protestants. And Protestants recognize the full validity of marriage by a judge or other civil official.

The Roman Catholic Church recognizes none of these ecumenical features of the American marriage system. Ordinarily, the Church refuses to recognize as valid the marriage of a Catholic before a Protestant clergyman or a civil official, and it will not permit the mixed marriage of a Catholic to a Protestant even before a priest, unless the Catholic party pledges to raise all children as Catholics. Even the forward-looking Second Vatican Council, in spite of tremendous pressure for reform, clung to the old Canon Law on marriage, divorce, and annulment, making it impossible for

Catholics whose marriage has failed to separate and start life over again with a new spouse.

This intransigence of Rome in the sexual field has made men forget that until recently Protestant policy on marriage was also petrified and archaic. England forbade the marriage of a man to his deceased wife's sister for several centuries, and the silly prohibition was not wiped out until 1907. England also made divorce almost impossible except for the rich until this century. In the United States, where divorce is a matter of state rather than federal law, many states forbade divorce throughout most of the nineteenth century. South Carolina, with its embattled fundamentalists, was the last state to permit divorce.

In New York State the law permitting divorce for one cause only, adultery, had become such a national scandal that even the Catholic Church finally consented to a change. Since then the movement toward reasoned liberalism in marriage and divorce has gone forward with astonishing speed. California now leads all the states in permitting divorce without a public, adversary brawl. The new scheme amounts to divorce by mutual consent, after due deliberation, and it is likely that this California pattern will spread contagiously because it fits the realities of modern marriage.

Where did church control of marriage come from? Catholic theologians assert that it came directly from God and Jesus Christ, and they cite the appropriate verses in the Bible fluently. But the verses do not establish the claim. Jesus never performed a marriage ceremony himself or prescribed any ecclesiastical forms for marriage. He is represented as having instituted "the sacrament of marriage" at a wedding in Cana which is described in John 2, but an examination of that simple story shows no sanction for any ceremonial practices or rules. Jewish weddings at that time were not priestly in character, and Jesus did not prescribe any new priestly powers for marriage. He was merely a guest at the wedding in Cana, and his chief accomplishment at the wedding was to manufacture six waterpots of wine out of water when the guests had run short of wine. Priestly exegetes have taken this simple narrative and expanded its meaning into a whole manual of marital usage.

Some of the elaborate apparatus for priestly control of marriage is quite recent. For about six hundred years the people of the Christian church required no priest at all to officiate at a marriage. Then priests gained new powers at the Council of Trent, and finally in the *Ne Temere* decree of 1907 the hierarchy made exclusive priestly participation a requirement for any marriage ceremony involving a Catholic. Officially the Catholic marriage rules are very harsh and absolute. Every Catholic who makes an "attempt" at marriage before a Protestant minister, Jewish rabbi, or civil judge is not married at all, and his children are bastards. In free America under a secular government many young Catholics defy such cruel laws and leave the Church. In Catholic countries like the Irish Republic or Spain the social as well as legal penalties are so severe that such escape is almost impossible.

The injustice of the narrow Catholic rules bears most heavily upon non-Catholics who wish to marry Catholics in a mixed-marriage ceremony. The Church will not permit such a marriage if the non-Catholic is treated as an equal. He must orally consign away the religion of all children, and usually he must take a course of instruction in the Catholic faith. If he is a Jew, he labors under a special discrimination called disparity of cult, which requires special consent from Rome before the marriage can be performed.

Fortunately, young Catholics by the thousands are defying such rules and marrying across creedal lines in spite of the penalties. Catholic writers have frequently admitted that the severity of the mixed-marriage rules is counterproductive and that the majority of children of mixed marriages end up outside of the Church. Probably the majority of younger priests would also like to see the mixed-marriage rules relaxed but they are powerless before their hierarchy in the Catholic system.

In the area of divorce the situation is equally

unpleasant for liberal Catholics and for those non-Catholics who would like to marry a Catholic. When the marriage of a Catholic fails, the Church ordinarily refuses to give such a Catholic the right to dissolve the marriage and remarry. There are a few technical exceptions to that rule, but they are minuscule. The penalty for an "attempt" at remarriage is excommunication, since the original marriage of a Catholic even to a syphilitic and insane murderer is considered eternal and binding in the eyes of God. Pope Paul went out of his way at the Second Vatican Council to reassert his personal intransigence on this point.

Paul's intransigence came into worldwide notice even during the Vatican Council when his own country, Italy, finally achieved after decades of political wrangling a "little divorce" law which gave suffering victims of mis-marriages some slight relief. The Pope argued that because of the 1929 Concordat between the Vatican and Mussolini the Italian people are permanently barred from applying any divorce legislation to Catholics unless the papacy consents. That Concordat gave the Vatican as an independent state treaty rights over the marriage of all Catholics in Italy—at least the Vatican claims that this is the meaning of the rather ambiguous language used. As I write these words, the Vatican and the government of Italy are locked in a bitter struggle on this issue. Meanwhile, the fate of more than a million separated spouses in Italy is at stake. They are living in open "sin" with new "wives" and "bastard" children while theologians argue with politicians over the sanctity of marriage.

The conservatives who claim that no Christian marriage can be dissolved under Christian law do not have any clear and unconditional authority for their claim. They are manufacturing scriptural certainties in an area of doubt. Jesus was a Jew, and in interpreting his words there is a reasonable presumption that he favored Jewish law unless he contradicted such law unequivocally. Jewish law permitted divorce for a number of reasons. When Jesus was asked by the Pharisees to state his policy on permissible divorce, he said in two places in the Gospels that he opposed it under all circumstances, and in two other places in those Gospels he declared that it was permissible in the case of adultery. His unconditional opposition to divorce is recorded in Mark 10:2-12 and Luke 16:18; his more liberal attitude is in Matthew 5:31-32 and 19:3-12.

In any case, such a critical problem as the indissolubility of all marriages cannot be solved by scriptural nit-picking. Millions of good men and women in the world make honest mistakes in marriage, and their civil rights demand that they should be given the power to throw off the old yoke and start life over again. A life sentence for all marital misfits seems to be cruel and unusual punishment.

We have mentioned in this chapter several of the great trouble areas of Christendom and sex in which, we believe, established Christianity has taken the wrong turn in dealing with family issues. There remain two other important questions, more or less related, concerning the authenticity and desirability of Christian attitudes in this area. To what extent was Jesus himself responsible for the lack of sexual realism in organized Christianity? Is not Christian, anti-sexual conservatism justified in spite of some of its extremist apostles by the reality of the threat to family life contained in our current relaxed sexual attitudes?

To attempt an answer to this first question: The weight of the evidence seems to favor the assumption that Jesus himself was a sexual conservative who endorsed a restrictive sexual standard of conduct. In Matthew 5:27 ff., he declared: "Ye have heard that it was said Thou shalt not commit adultery, but I say unto you that everyone that looketh on a woman to lust after her hath committed adultery with her already in his heart." If that admonition were applied to all Christian men everywhere, Peter would have very few male applicants at the pearly gates.

The eunuch story about Jesus in Matthew 19:12 is even more extreme than the lust story. There Jesus, being badgered by the Pharisees about sex and divorce, and having urged sexual abstinence in certain cases, finally says: "Not all men can receive this saying, but they to whom it is given. For there are eunuchs that were so born from their mother's womb, and there are eunuchs that were made eunuchs by men, and there are eunuchs that made themselves eunuchs for the kingdom of heaven's sake. He that is able to receive it, let him receive it."

For seventeen centuries this unfortunate verse has been quoted by celibate supporters of Augustine, Origen, and their kind as the divine sanction for the abnormal condition called celibacy. It was even cited in an official document of Vatican II as propaganda for "virginity or celibacy undertaken for the sake of the kingdom of heaven." Pope Paul used it as his principal documentary when he issued his famous 1967 encyclical *Sacerdotalis Caelibatus*.

There are, of course, many passages in the New Testament which suggest that Jesus had a liberal point of view on sex. He dealt freely with women of doubtful reputation. His admonition to the woman taken in adultery (John 8:3-11), "Go and sin no more," is the admonition of a realistic and merciful teacher who simultaneously brushed off the hypocrites with the rebuke: "He that is without sin among you, let him first cast a stone at her." His willingness to accept an alabaster cruse of ointment from a female sinner indicated broadmindedness.

But these stories are fragments. There is no direct reference to Jesus' sexuality anywhere in the New Testament, and it is probably correct to say that his total view on sex was routine and conventional. Since the dominant thought of his ministry was that the world was rapidly approaching the end, there seemed to be no time for joy in sex. Sex for joy was utterly absent in his teaching. He urged faithfulness between husband and wife, condemnation of all adultery, and consecration of the family to the coming kingdom.

What of Jesus' own sexual life? Was he a virgin? Was he a homosexual partner of John, "the beloved disciple," as many authors have suggested? Was he married himself to a secret wife or to a young wife who disappeared from his later ministry?

For a long time such questions have been dismissed as sensational or insulting by biblical scholars. But one scholar has recently broken through the taboos about Jesus and sex; he is a Presbyterian minister, Dr. William A. Phipps, whose book *Was Jesus Married?* has been published by Harper and Row. He is not a sensation-monger but a professor of Religion and Philosophy at Davis and Elkins College in West Virginia. While his conditional answer to his title is nobody knows, he has marshaled an impressive mass of evidence to show that Jesus *might* have had a real sexual life entirely unknown to us. His entire life from boyhood to young manhood consisted of "hidden years." The legend of his appearance in the temple at the age of twelve is probably nothing more than a legend. In the void of silence surrounding his marriageable years, Jesus had plenty of time to marry and raise a family. Perhaps he remained celibate, perhaps not. His anti-sexual image may have been in part created by the anti-sexual Church Fathers who came after him. That is about all that we can say about the sexual mystery of Jesus.

The other great question about Christianity and sex must have an equally equivocal answer. Do current relaxed sexual standards justify conservative Christian reactions? Does old-fashioned Christianity have any adequate answers for a sexually wild generation?

Certainly it must be admitted that the Western family is in a more shaky position today than it has ever been during recorded history. Copulation outside of marriage is transforming our sexual mores with astonishing speed. Virginity in the young is becoming more and more unusual. Divorce is on the increase and permissiveness is the rule rather than the exception. Granted that the new generation probably gets more joy out of sex than our Victorian grandparents did, is this kind of instant happiness lasting?

The honest answer to all these agonizing doubts and questions seems to be that Christianity no longer has an answer. The pulpit has relied for so long on scriptural generalizations about purity and sin that it is not now capable of supplying a moral framework for sex for the younger generation. If marriage and love are to be saved, and I think they are both worth saving, the salvation must come not from organized religion but from plain people not motivated by any religious dogma, and from secular prophets and scholars who make use of all the learning that social and physical science has to offer.

6 Wanted:
A Person Who Calls
Himself God

(Young Self—1917)

I was musing the other night by the fire while
the pine logs crackled musically. . . .

There came a very gentle tapping at the
door. I thought at first it was our pet dog
gotten loose from the stable where he sleeps at
night, but when I went to the door and
opened it, the cold November wind blew in
without any dog. Startled, I looked into the
darkness and saw an old, white-haired man
crouched by the doorway. There was an

expression of real terror on his face, and, as I opened the door farther, he slipped in and crouched in the corner.

"What is the matter?" I asked in some astonishment. "What are you doing in those rags on such a night?"

"They are looking for me," he whispered. I noticed that he was trembling violently.

"Who is looking for you?" I asked.

"Everybody," he replied. "I guess I am what you call a criminal. I have committed more crimes than any other person in the world, and wherever I go somebody is trying to kill me."

As the door blew shut, he jumped as if he had been shot. Then he stared at me so unblinkingly that I thought he must be suffering from some mental disease. Finally I pulled a chair up to the fireplace and asked him to sit down and tell me his story. He was suspicious at first, but after we had warmed our hands together he seemed to thaw out. Then he told me this strange tale.

"I am God." I jumped a little, but he looked at me unperturbed. "That is what everybody does when I tell them my name," he said, "but you see they don't understand."

I smiled and waved my hand for him to go on.

"I am very old," he said. The deep wrinkles in his face and the long white hair falling to his shoulders bore evidence of the fact.

"I don't know when I was born, but it was a

long time ago. For a good many centuries I lived in big trees and mountains and clouds where I had a delightful time. Then I went up above the clouds where it is cold, very cold. Occasionally I came down to special celebrations like miracles and earthquakes, but most of the time it has been very lonely. I was glad when they brought me down to earth and I hoped at first that folks would make friends of me, but they didn't. They don't seem to know how human I am. In almost every spot in the world now I am subject to hanging or electrocution."

"But my friend," I asked, "what are all the terrible things you have done?"

For answer he pulled out from his bosom a long white printed bill. It was so long that it seemed to unroll itself for miles and miles before I saw the end. He noted my surprise with evident pride.

"Read it," he said, "and you will see why I am wanted at every bar of judgment in the world."

I took it eagerly and began to read:

Wanted—A person who calls himself God,

Variously described as a tree, a cloud, ether and a man,

When last seen was on top of Sinai.

He is wanted by the criminal court of humanity for the commission of the following crimes:

He created Adam, and then tempted him to destruction.

He drowned several million innocent people for disagreeing with some of his bigoted Hebrew prophets.

He wanted to destroy the world but was prevented from doing so by the sacrificing charity of Jesus.

He made Judas a betrayer and then sent him to hell for playing true to his part.

He has murdered many millions of his children by famines, fires, earthquakes and plagues.

He has been the leader of every gang of national murderers from the first tribal blood feud to the recent European holocaust.

He has made the human race ignorant, diseased and hateful—

"Yes, yes," interrupted God, pointing a long bony finger at the last indictment I had read. "That at least is true."

His finger touched my hand and it seemed to burn with a terrible sting. I jumped up in my agony.

My wife was laughing at me, for a spark from the fireplace had fallen upon my hand while I was asleep.

Since that dream I have thought a good deal about God and found the subject rather profitable. The religious teacher often scorns the simple, common-sense questions about God which occur to any man when he begins to think. The idea of the fatherhood of God is usually treated with the obscurity of philosophical terms or the soporific of personal raptures. If a preacher ever recovers from these evasive treatments of the subject of God, he asks some strangely naive but strangely penetrating questions.

If God is my Father, why does he leave me alone at so many crises of my life?

If God is my Father, why does he not want to live on more intimate terms with his children?

If God is my Father, why does he allow one-half of the world to kill the other half in his name?

To put our questions in the words attributed to Sydney Smith, "Damn the solar system—bad light—planets too distant—pestered with comets—feeble contrivance—could make a better with great ease."

Now the common-sense reply to these queries is almost too simple to record, but I have never heard it effectively combated. If I call any man my father, I assume that he is something like me, that he belongs to my race and family. I assume that he cares enough for me to guard me as much as possible from disease, crime and disaster. If an American father who had the power to save his son from dying in a burning house allowed him to be destroyed without an attempt to save him., he would be branded as a legal and moral criminal. Yet God took the flower of my family and burned her to death one day in a cellar because she inadvertently tipped over a kerosene lamp.

The popular attitude after such a disaster is to "cling bravely to my faith." In that way millions of Russian peasants clung to faith in their czar after he had shown himself utterly heedless of their welfare. For myself I cannot dodge the issue. I cannot continue to believe that God is my father or the father of the human race when he betrays so little care for the lives and welfare of his poverty-stricken, diseased and helpless children.

When the evils of the world weaken our faith in the fatherhood of God, there comes with the weakening a reaction toward optimism. We pass in review the many splendid privileges of the modern man, the delights of nature's beauty, and the friendship of kindly and honest souls who make life rich and happy by their unselfishness. "How," we ask in this optimistic mood, "how can a God who is careless or cold give mankind all these blessings?"

But the truth is that the blessings which God bestows upon humanity are not half so prolific or beneficial in proportion to his supposed power as the kindnesses which the average earthly father bestows upon his child. The earthly father sacrifices himself to keep the child warm and well-fed and happy. The earthly mother goes into the valley of the shadow to bring the soul of her child into the world. Where outside of the fatuous fictions of theology can we find the love of God manifested as superior to this? If a child is suddenly left to the exclusive mercies of a heavenly father, how clearly superior the earthly father appears!

We cannot evade the truism that a good father will not make some of his children wealthy and some of them diseased and poor, if he has the power to make them all happy. If God is the all-powerful father of the human race, he must be referred to the Society for the Prevention of Cruelty to Children.

There is current in some quarters today a certain brand of agnostic optimism which passes for faith in the fatherhood of God. Our healthy animal natures will not allow us to be pessimistic all the time. We are surrounded by people who have strong religious convictions and whose convictions unconsciously influence us in our judgments. So, when we are asked to believe in the fatherhood of God, we are honest enough to say that we do not know anything about God and we do not believe anything in particular about him, but we hope for the best. We are agnostics but not cynics. Whatever is the Power that controls the universe, we are bound that we shall deal with It (or Him) cheerfully and without distrust. The world is a pretty good place to live in in spite of all the earthquakes and fires. You can call this faith if you want to.

This determination to be cheerful plays an amazingly large part in the faith of the people. Tennyson in his *In Memoriam* reaches antireligious conclusions and then sinks back from sheer exhaustion to a cheerful and innocuous faith. The desire of his heart is so strong that all else is forgotten. He dare not look into the darkness of the night and declare, "I do not know." He loves human life and human hope too much to be so cruelly candid. He allows the tremendous emotional power of a great desire to bring him into a mood of exaltation, and the power of that desire he calls "faith."

Is it not so with the preacher? He does not stop to analyze the idea of the fatherhood of God. He is embarked upon the task of finding a solution for the world riddle, a solution that will make him and the world happy. In the joy of doing effective work his critical faculty is dulled and forgotten, so far forgotten indeed that he comes to regard any hostile criticism of religion as indecent. The inexpressible yearning he has to "know God" is exalted to the level of faith, and imparted with all the power of his being to his fellow men. He prays "Our Father" so often that the habit becomes an unshakable belief.

He does not stop to reason that if this world were really conducted by a beneficent father he would not have to pray at all, and there would be no unutterably horrible pain to explain away.

But a new generation of clergymen is arising which insists on discussing candidly the problem of God. Many sturdy-minded preachers of our own day are trying to adjust the idea of the fatherhood of God to the facts of science and common sense. They are seeking to put a new content in the term "Father," and still ally themselves with the Christian church. What they have really done is to take over two conceptions of God that are quite foreign to Christianity.

"God," says the modern liberal thinker, "is Universal Life inspired with purpose and moving forward toward better things. All things are a part of God and in various degrees inspired with his purpose."

Such a belief comes naturally to the man who realizes that the old tribal God of the Jews is too small for our modern world and contradictory to the teachings of evolution. Obviously some mighty force is working in nature and in human life, bringing things into a rough unity, creating and destroying human life and keeping rigid the great natural laws. The existence of that force is necessary to explain the largeness of life and its multitude of complexities.

So when the modern thinker describes God as the Life Force and each one of us as the "children of the universal God who is not separate from material life but directly identified with it and expressing Himself through every manifestation of life," we feel that we have found a belief that can agree with our common-sense judgments and what little we know of science.

But is this kind of God our father? Only by

the most inexcusable distortion of the term. The fact that I am a part or product of God does not prove that I am his son. I cannot claim that the Life takes any special interest in me or that I am a more significant part than other parts. The Life is also the father of monkeys and toads and volcanoes.

When we are children, we think of God as a great, white-bearded man, or as the enlargement of our father. When we are older, we still think of him as a man with certain powers of "spiritual" extension. But the reflection of maturity will bring us inevitably to this conclusion, that we have no more right to call God a man or a person than an orange has the right to call the orange tree "The Great Orange." The relation of part to the whole is not the relation of child to father. Only our animal limitations lead us to think of the universe as human.

So the first idea of God which the modern man naturally accepts is too large for fatherhood. The universe no doubt contains qualities of love and friendship, but those qualities are buried deep and quite lost sight of in the great mass of mechanical forces that compose nature. The blind men who felt the elephant described it variously as a wall, a rope and a tree. The Christian enthusiast who takes a few characteristics of the World Force and considers them apart from the blind and a moral course of life is feeling only part of the elephant. God as Universal Being has even fewer fatherly qualities than the elephant has of rope. To describe him as father shows an unforgivable weakness in allowing our wishes to blind our reason. He is not "good'" any more than he is green. He is not our father any more than the air we breathe.

My gentle reader will be shocked by these views, for you are no doubt accustomed to very skillful word-juggling about the personality of God. It is a subject easy to becloud by a few skillful phrases. To satisfy the average congregation the preacher must at least seem to reconcile the Christian idea of God as a personal being in the sky who came down to beget a child by a Jewish virgin, with the modern idea of a Progressive World Force. The beclouding and the fusion are done in this way:

"We see in the universe Unity, Thought and Feeling. These are the great characteristics of personality and cannot be manifested apart from personality. So the Universal God must be personal. He is the Father of us all, for from Him we gain all the elements of our being. Our religious consciousness is valid for He manifests consciousness in the evolution of the world-process."

Now the thinness of this reasoning can be seen when we record its opposite.

"We see in the universe Chaos, Ignorance and Cruelty. These are the characteristics of an Insane Devil and cannot be manifested apart from the phenomenon of personality. So the Universal Devil must be personal. Our religious consciousness is invalid because the Universal Devil does not reveal in the course of evolution any consciousness akin to our own."

And we arrive exactly where we started.

Whether a man believes in the goodness of Life or its essential deviltry depends upon the condition of his digestion and the place he occupies in society. If his digestion is good and his place in society is secure, the preacher has little difficulty in persuading him that the Great Power which he vaguely believes in is the personal Father of Jesus Christ.

But for myself I must recognize that the Universal Power indicated by the findings of modern science, whether that Power is divine or devilish, does not fit the description and does not accord with the prophecies of Jesus. It would be culpably inaccurate and evasive if I sought to convince the people that the moving force of the solar system is the same God who was about to destroy the world between 25 and 50 A.D. and set up a kingdom for his son Jesus.

But what of religious experience? Thousands of honest men and women have gained a "personal knowledge" of God, and there is a growing desire among all variety of thinkers to explain this experience in rational terms. That experience ranges all the way from the hysteria of a Pentecostal camp-meeting to the personal prayers of a great philosopher.

To meet this necessity there has grown up a different idea of God. Instead of making God omnipotent and universal we must make him intimate and tangible. God is made up of the combined spirit of the faithful believers. He is the group spirit of the mob. He is the medium of consciousness, the inclusive consciousness which binds our minds together. He is the finite god whom we feel in the enthusiasm of the great revival, in the onward rush of a mighty army, even in the mad blood-lust of an infuriated mob. There is something more in every group of people than the individual mind of each person. That something is the Common Spirit with which men commune when they have religious experience.

"Where two or three are gathered together in my name, there am I in the midst of them." This promise of Jesus is taken up by the believer in the new god and a new meaning put into it. Where two or three are gathered together, they create the god-spirit for themselves. They are reborn in the realm of a new existence, larger and nobler than their old life.

This god is union-made. He fires the heart of the agitator with passion for redeeming his class. He thrills the soul of the Fifth Avenue rector with a like passion for preserving all the niceties of upper-class morals. He is the spirit who makes new decalogues on the Sinai of Public Opinion.

This god is the social conscience of the people. He expresses his will in the moral laws of man. He grows with men, suffers with them, and saves them through the tangible forces of social communion.

He is not responsible for the world's earthquakes, fires and murders, for he does not control the solar system.

It does not take a moment's thought to decide that this god of modern reflection is not our father. He is a child of humanity whom we have made out of the texture of our own consciousness. He cannot be omnipotent and he cannot explain the meaning of life. But he can explain those heart-yearnings and vague communions which we have learned to call religious experience. He is our spiritual confessor in a very real sense, for to him we take our judgments, sorrows and sins, and by communion with him we purify our souls of selfish ways.

With us the personality of this god has been associated with the personality of Jesus because Jesus has been identified with all the best ideals of our common life. But the association has been purely accidental. The same kind of god leads the pilgrims to Mecca and stirs the spirit of the Hindu fakir, and like the Christian, the Mohammedan and the Buddhist believe that this god is necessarily associated with their favorite prophets. But when the world has passed beyond the worship of any one prophet, this god will still reign.

The transition to belief in the god of common spirit has already been partly accomplished. The truth is that the world for a long time has been giving only a lip profession to God the Father. There is a hopeless confusion in our thinking of God as Universal Force and god as common spirit. The average man shakes up the mixture and affixes the Christian label "Father," but only in the wildest moments of evangelistic rapture does he assume that any spirit is taking personal charge of his life.

Bernard Shaw has pointed out that what men really believe can be discovered not from their formal creeds but from the assumptions on which they act. The test when applied to the human race shows that we have long ago abandoned the idea of the fatherhood of God and have adopted a double idea of God as Universal Force and God as personal spirit. In the natural course of our thinking I believe we have hit upon the truth.

I believe in both of the gods I have described above, for both of them are necessary to explain life. Science points the way to a Universal Force which makes order possible. Personal experience and the teachings of modern psychology indicate the existence of a god of group-consciousness. These gods bear some relation to each other but that relation is not an intimate one. They cannot be consolidated into one by a trick of intellectual gymnastics.

When we have thus escaped from the idea of God's fatherhood, there should be no pretense of being Christian. Jesus Christ has not given us our God nor will we ever be able to go back to the God of Jesus. Little Judea, alive with Oriental imaginings, shut in from mighty Western currents, has given us many mystical treasures, but she cannot give us a god adequate for the world of modern knowledge. Each era must choose its own gods, and the time has at last come when we are ready to acknowledge the people's part in the choice.

For myself, the only god who means much to me will be the god of our common opinion. He tells me what is right and wrong. He is made in my image. With him I am willing to go into the future ignorant of the Great Riddle but still unafraid.

(Old Self—1974)

In the 57 years since the Young Blanshard recorded the above conversation with God, that estimable deity has declined in popular standing so far that he is scarcely recognizable. God has become god, demoted by historians and by-passed by psychoanalysts. And the Blanshard of 1974 is no longer willing to describe his foggy and sentimental God of 1917 as still existing.

The Christian God has become the constant

target of attack even from within the Christian community, an attack almost as severe as that of the atheists. Sigmund Freud in *The Future of an Illusion* concluded that "the father nucleus" lies behind the idea of God, and that "religion is comparable to a childhood neurosis." He added that "the religious ideas which profess to be dogmas are not the residue of experience or the final result of reflection; they are illusions, fulfillments of the oldest, strongest and most insistent wishes of mankind." His attack was directed not only against Christianity but against all religion: "We must characterize the religions of mankind as a mass delusion."

Paul Tillich, the most eminent Protestant theologian of this century, buried Christianity under an avalanche of ambiguous words. He virtually defined the Christian God out of existence by saying that "God is being itself, not *a* being," and added: "It is as atheistic to affirm the existence of God as it is to deny it." All of which reminds me of Oscar Wilde who once said that "to be intelligible is to be found out." Tillich was not found out very promptly because competing scholars were frightened by his ambiguities, and they threw their stones from theological glass houses.

Came recently the "God Is Dead" theologians, on both sides of the Atlantic, who sought to make a faithless faith out of ambiguous Christian faith. They created endless confusion without supplying any new answers. Perhaps their greatest accomplishment was to de-bunk theological orthodoxy by showing that its terms are full of double meanings.

Intellectually the Western world is still living in a state of confusion as to God and god. There is no longer any clear consensus on the subject of divine existence. If opinion polls are to be believed, the overwhelming majority of the American people are still willing to say that they believe in God. Apparently they believe more completely than the people of any other large nation. But the statistics do not tell all the truth because the meaning of religious terms is steeped in ambiguity. Sometimes the ambiguity seems to be deliberately created by the theologians because they know that plain-speaking would reveal their beliefs as absurd. Today a belief in God often means nothing more than an acknowledgement of the existence of some over-arching physical power in the universe, and such an acknowledgement can be accepted by a complete materialist.

The foggy and condescending attitude toward a foggy deity was satirized by Anthony Towne in the *New York Times* during the "God Is Dead" controversy in 1966 when he wrote an "Obituary for God" in the style of the *New York Times*. One choice part reads: "Public reaction in this country was perhaps summed up by an elderly retired streetcar conductor in Passaic, New Jersey, who said: 'I never met him, of course, never even saw him. But from what I heard I guess he was a real nice fellow. Tops.' "

A Harris poll taken in 1965 indicated that 97 per cent of the American people "believed in God." But what does that profession imply? What kind of God? In 1949 a Catholic scholar tried to reach realities in this area by taking a careful poll of the members of the American Sociological Society as to their belief in the nature and existence of God. About 64 per cent of them gave some kind of affirmative response to the world "God" but when the figures were broken down it was revealed that 35 per cent defined God as Impersonal Force, 18 per cent classified themselves as "agnostic" or "no comment," and only 29 per cent accepted the idea of God as a "Personal Being." It would seem that acceptance of a Personal Being is the minimum requirement for Christian faith in a Christian God, and, reasoning on that basis, fewer than one-third of the sociologists questioned could be correctly described as Christians.

I think it is fair to say that while Americans are officially continuing to profess God-beliefs, they are rapidly drifting away from any real faith in the God of any particular creed. God language and creed language no longer create much public interest. Theological disputes often appear to the younger generation to be irrelevant hair-splitting.

Look, for example, at the greatest of all Christian creeds, that adopted at the Council of Nicea in 325. Here it is in the form used in a Catholic high-school textbook in the United States:

"We believe in One God, the Father Almighty, Creator of all things visible and invisible: and in One Lord Jesus Christ, the Son of God, begotten as the only begotten of the Father, that is, from the essence of the Father, God from God, Light from Light, true God from true God, begotten, not created, consubstantial with the Father, through Whom all things were made, both in heaven and earth; Who for us men and for our salvation came down and was incarnate, was made Man: Who suffered and rose again on the third day, ascended into heaven, and shall come again to judge the living and the dead; and in the Holy Ghost.—But those who say: 'There was a time when He was not, and before he was begotten He was not, and He came into existence out of what was not;' or who say: 'He is of a different nature and essence from the Father,' or 'the Son of God is created or capable of change,' let them be anathema."

What practical man in the twentieth century is interested in whether Jesus was "consubstantial with the Father" and whether he existed "before he was begotten" and whether he was "begotten, not created"? Yet the Catholic authorities are correct in saying that this is a vital part of Christianity. Somewhere there must be an absolute minimum of faith in a Christian God if anything called Christianity is to exist, and these horrendous and seemingly irrelevant speculations in the Creed seem to represent the nearest thing we can find in Christian history to an essence of Christianity. Belief in a prayer-hearing Divine Father who actually communicates with His children, even if the communication is only a one-way street, would seem to be the final residue of Christian faith required in a skeptical world.

I think that the decline in the belief in an exclusive, personal Christian God can be explained in part by the growth of studies in comparative religion. College students now have the opportunity of hearing about the non-American world, not as a colonial area of false faiths to be conquered by righteous Christianity but as an interesting sociological field of exploration. The imperialist missionary atmosphere of the nineteenth century is disappearing along with the expensive and largely fruitless evangelistic institutions it fostered. Even Christian theological seminaries sometimes give equal treatment to "foreign" faiths other than Christianity, and frequently the gods of these other religions appear more attractive than Yahweh.

Robert Ingersoll once said that "an honest God is the noblest work of man." This reversal of the standard myth that God makes man is the final step in disillusion for many of the present generation. It may be described as the ultimate in skepticism or the ultimate in "creative religion." It marks the conviction of millions of honest doubters that man must take charge of his own faith.

Of course, the most fundamental reason why the Christian God is on the defensive in modern thought is that almost nothing in Christianity explains the universe, either the physical universe or the dynamic brain of man or the moral universe. We are no longer living in a tribal world ruled over by a tribal God. It is a world of planets and quasars many billion light-years away, and almost nothing in this new universe seems to fit the concepts of that Yahweh who herded all the animals in the world into a single ark during the Flood.

The theory that there is a two-way loving binding man and God seems doubly questionable in such a world. If God is omnipotent and also loves mankind, why is it that, as John Stuart Mill once pointed out: "Nearly all the things which men are hanged or imprisoned for doing to one another are nature's everyday performance"? As a character invented by Voltaire has put it: "If he cannot prevent evil, he is not almighty, if he will not, he is cruel." In any case the argument against God's lack of goodness profoundly affects the argument for his existence. Who wants to believe in the existence of a deity who creates 58 species of termites in the United States? As to man's alleged love for the Christian Triune God, how could any rational man love a Father who sent his Son down to the world to be crucified for sins which that Son never committed, and who provided a Judas to betray him?

The silliest myth about the Christian deity is that this omnipotent God actually loves each Christian. Would a loving father refuse to speak clearly to his child if he loved him? Would a loving father fail to make himself visible to his children? Would a loving father produce infantile vegetables destined to slobber their way through lifetimes of idiocy?

As to the mathematics of the Trinity, no one has improved on Robert Ingersoll's summary on the subject, taken from his lecture on "The Foundations of Faith." He said: "Christ, according to the faith, is the second person of the Trinity, the Father being the first and the Holy Ghost the third. Each of these three persons is God. Christ is his own father and his own son. The Holy Ghost is neither father nor son, but both. The Son was begotten by the Father, but existed before he was begotten—just the same before as after. Christ is just as old as his Father, and the Father is just as young as his Son. The Holy Ghost proceeded from the Father and Son, but was equal to the Father and Son before he proceeded, that is to say, before he existed, but he is of the same age of the other two.

"So it is declared that the Father is God,

and the Son God and the Holy Ghost God, and that these three Gods make one God.

"According to the celestial multiplication table, once one is three, and three times one is one, and according to heavenly subtraction if we take two from three, three are left. The addition is equally peculiar, if we add two to one we have but one. Each one is equal to himself and the other two. Nothing ever was, nothing ever can be more perfectly idiotic and absurd than the dogma of the Trinity."

We shall see later that the Christian's dress-parade faith which he mentions to an opinion pollster makes little difference in his daily life. As to a personal God, he never declaims, as LaPlace did to Napoleon, that "I have, sir, no need for that hypothesis," but he acts on the assumption that his deity does not actually interfere with the routines of daily life. He knows that he must carve out his own destiny for himself. He uses the idea of God as a kind of decorative and poetic addition to his real thinking. God, he supposes, may be Something Out There, or Up There or All Around Us. The location is not important, and he leaves spiritual geography to the theologians.

7 The Unimportance of Being Christian

(Young Self—1917)

I talked not long ago with one of America's greatest Jewish leaders as he sat by the fireside with his family. His was an ideal home full of enlightenment and love. It was what we have learned to call a "Christian home." As we talked together of the problems of labor and social reform that confront us, I realized the true nobility and unselfishness of the man. Then the thought came to me, "How ridiculous it would seem for me to say that he was damned for his unbelief while I was saved by my Christianity." He had more of love and patience and idealism than I would ever have. He could convert me to Judaism sooner than I could win him to Christianity.

But I did not try to convert him to Christianity because I realized the unimportance of being Christian.

What I felt has been tacitly agreed upon by most Christians for a long time. Proselytizing for the Christian religion has become a lost art. I mean real proselytizing. When young men and women who have been surrounded by church influences all their lives finally reach the age of decision, their entrance into organized Christianity is as automatic and inevitable as their entrance into society. In fact it is little else but an entrance into moral society under the careful guidance of anxious parents. Put the same kind of children with the same kind of parents into Arabia and the apples would fall as readily into Mohammedan baskets.

When Billy Sunday preaching in a Christian nation after Christianity has been on trial for nearly two thousand years succeeds in winning several thousand converts to Christianity he is hailed as a remarkable teacher. He is a remarkable teacher. His success stands out in striking contrast to the failure of almost every other evangelist who has had the courage to preach Christianity in all its nakedness.

It requires no special investigation to

discover that most people in America are genuinely indifferent to all that conversion implies. They are quite heedless of the preachers' solemn question, "Where will you spend eternity?" They do not know where they will spend eternity and they are quite certain that Christianity will not enlighten them in the matter. In the South and especially among the foreign workingmen who operate many of our greatest industries, hundreds are buried without funerals, utterly scornful even in their grief of the churches' teaching concerning life and death.

In opposition to this widespread indifference there are two classes of preachers who are successful in their proselytizing, modern and genial pastors who never preach Christianity, and the vaudeville evangelists who by their magnetic power shock people out of their normal littleness.

I belong to the first class. I have converted many people to my own conceptions of morality and religion with the help of biblical phrases and the authority which the church has given me, but I have never converted any one to the religion of Jesus Christ. For a long time I thought that I was a Christian evangelist. Now I know that there are very few Christian evangelists, and that the astute businessmen and special pleaders who fill our city pulpits are converting men not to Christianity but to certain moral standards of optimism, honesty, self-confidence and ambition that will guarantee their success in the present social system. If I, as a city pastor, should suddenly declare that unless my congregation abandoned their earthly work, took no thought for the morrow, trusted in God so much that the food supply should be obtained by prayer to the Father who promised through his Son that everyone who asked should receive, I would instantly be asked to resign.

Men would say that I was preaching insanity. The tragedy is that they would be right, and I would be Christian.

But the professional evangelists who are attempting to defend Christianity are a far more interesting study than the sensible city pastors. They are the true successors of St. Paul, earnest, enthusiastic, and successful, because they have reduced religion to a compact formula which even the most ignorant cannot mistake. How delightfully simple this formula is! Believe in the Lord Jesus Christ and thou shalt be saved. For the rest, be good!

The character of these evangelists betrays them. Even the laity is beginning to be suspicious of that character. I have met many evangelists and heard many more give forth the sound and fury of gospel heat, and I have never yet discovered an effective evangelist who had a good education coupled with sane and careful judgment. The foremost representative of proselytizing Christianity are emotional calliopes who play upon the ignorance and emotional hunger of their audiences. Some of them are sincere with the sincerity created by personal power and exciting success—it is hard for successful men to disbelieve in themselves and their mission. Some of them are sincere with the sincerity of unadulterated ignorance. Many of them are emotionally and morally rotten, afraid to face the simplest doubt with candid analysis.

The character of the revivalists throws suspicion upon the value of their message. It is not the falsehood of that message which impresses the observer so much as the unimportance of it. That unimportance is due at least partially to the remoteness of the message of the Bible.

The Bible is not only incomprehensible to the average man: It is incomprehensible to most scholars. This is not because of any unusual depth of reasoning but because it is the work of contradictory, untrained minds, speaking a language which we do not completely understand, and setting forth a view of life which we can appreciate only by the systematic stretching of a trained imagination. We cannot understand the Bible unless we can "put ourselves back" into Palestine and catch a glimpse of the world as it appeared to Jewish prophets and priests. And when, after years of special training, the scholar succeeds in realizing something of the real biblical viewpoint, he sees how little vitality there is in the message which ancient Jewish sages bring to us.

Let me make my own confession in regard to the Bible. I have never enjoyed reading it until there was placed in my hands a modern English version that put in clear, twentieth-century phrases the chapters that in the old King James version had regularly put me to sleep on Sunday afternoon. The enjoyment then was short-lived. The effect of this modern-speech version was startling. When compared with the works of almost any successful writer of my experience, the Bible stood out as ineffably dull not only in its subject matter but in its style. How pedantic were the epigrams of Jesus! How easily the American preacher could equal the letters of St. Paul if he chose to write letters to his flock! How puerile were the rhapsodies of Revelation!

When I saw how outworn superstition was freely mixed with mystical epigram, I was tempted to throw the whole thing away. But the deep, bass voice of my professor of homiletics kept ringing in my ears: "Young men, use the Scriptures! No book in the world has such power over the thoughts and imagination of men as the Bible. If you want to convince men of your opinions, use the Bible."

So I have used the Bible, although I have used it with an increasing sense of its real unimportance. I have seen many lives transformed by faith in the Bible but I have never yet seen a life transformed by the Bible. The distinction is important. The bones of St. Anna have never yet killed a germ or strengthened a muscle, but the absolute conviction of scores of people that the strengthening and germ-killing would be accomplished by the bones has sent back many an invalid to his home healed and jubilant.

When a careful study is made of these people to whom the Bible is preeminently important, it will be found in almost every case that they are either professionals who must use the Bible in the development of their careers or ignorant people whose range of reading is so limited that the narratives and exhortations of the Bible are interesting. Because the Bible was the only serious and vital literature in so many thousands of the homes of our grandfathers it became for them a genuinely sacred book. It contained the only philosophy and poetry they ever read. In a life of endless monotony and commonplaceness, it was the only thing that demanded their reverence.

But with expanding knowledge, the Bible is gradually taking its more natural place with the other dust-covered articles on the parlor table or the bottom shelf of the family bookcase. Nehemiah, Jehoshaphat, and their kind are described in the Sunday school and then promptly forgotten. In the life of

America the Bible has already become an unimportant symbol, like a literary rosary, to be purchased and occasionally thumbed through but seldom to be read.

There is another and much more significant indication of the unimportance of Christianity in our time. The moral ideas of the race when frankly examined show practically no dependence upon the maintenance of Christianity.

Even in the questions of personal morals we do not follow distinctively Christian standards. The reason is that there are no Christian standards that can be effectively used in solving our ordinary moral problems.

If I consult the teachings of Jesus in regard to wine-drinking, I cannot discover whether I should be a total abstainer or not. Jesus did not know anything about American saloons. If I am anxious to know whether a divorced person can be married again, I find that the teachings of Jesus are ambiguous. Jesus was never married and he knew nothing of syphilis, low wages for working girls or the feminist movement. If I hesitate before entering the army and ask myself, "Is it possible for a Christian to be a soldier?" I find that Jesus can readily be made into a Quaker pacifist or a terrible fighter for all just causes. If I turn to the teachings of Jesus to find standards for honesty while earning a living, I find nothing beyond vague moral generalizations. Jesus knew nothing of moderr trusts, cut-throat competition and business honesty.

In the absence of definite Christian standards of morality, Christianity becomes merely a label for the particular moral system we want to endorse. No one can tell the world what Christianity really is, so everybody's religious business becomes nobody's religious business. What Christianity really is becomes unimportant. What the moral habits of the race are become all-important.

The thing we call Christianity will live for many centuries because it has succeeded in gathering unto itself the greatest moral qualities of the race and in using those qualities to bolster up an antiquated analysis of life and an institution that still dominates our moral horizon. So it has become a mixture of the most practical and noble truths with the most ridiculous deceptions. In the same breath we are asked to believe that we should love our neighbors, and that a certain fish swallowed Jonah and kept him in the submarine stateroom for three days. We are asked to accept the gospel of peace, and to believe that peace can come only through the belief by all humanity that God became completely incarnate in a certain Jewish prophet who lived many centuries ago.

As we confront this queer, impossible mixture, we cannot feel that it is important for any man to be a Christian. Obviously, the one important task of our time is to work for that society based upon more equal opportunity which is the ideal of all men whose faces "are turned toward the light." When we have glimpsed this larger vision, we cannot help but recognize the real irrelevancy of Christian proselytizing.

But the unimportance of being Christian does not include the unimportance of having churches. Quite apart from its function as an agent for the Christian Gospel the church is an organization of human beings met together for the purpose of reflection, service, and fellowship. In the vast arid desert of our unorganized life any church that brings the people together in fellowship is doing much for human life.

The old village tavern taught the people of the countryside what they knew of gossip, manners and politics. That social function was connected with the flowing bowl, but even the temperance reformer must recognize that the old tavern supplied a fundamental social need of the community. It brought men from loneliness into comradeship at a time when no other institution served that purpose. It taught men to know one another and to know themselves. It laid the basis of democracy.

So the church is helping the cause of democracy by bringing men under one roof who think and talk together of the common moral problems of the race. It is often dominated by class interests and unspeakably hypocritical, but to the man who observes *all*, life *is* dominated by class interests and unspeakably hypocritical. The church is no worse and probably a little better than most of our institutions. It is the only moral forum in thousands of communities; it is the most natural meeting-ground for those who are striving to do good. Until we have a better forum for the development of a people's philosophy and ethics, blessed be the church!

It is upon this rock that the enemy of the church most often founders. He denounces the church and praises what he calls "real Christianity." If he had studied the situation, his attitude would be just the reverse.

I have become an enemy of the Christian church but not an enemy of the church. I believe in the church but deny Christianity. I believe in the church not because of what it is today but because of the possibilities of a great temple of religious aspiration and moral reflection in the midst of a community whose thoughts are bent on petty things.

Ostensibly the church was built on Christianity, but it is now built upon something far more profound. Its real foundation is the craving for fellowship and the universal desire of men to know the secrets of life. The real basis of the public school is not White's *Arithmetic* or any other particular textbook, but the desire of the people for general learning.

Likewise the church. Eject Christianity (as it has already been partially ejected), substitute the religion and morals that each community works out for itself and you have a church 𝗆 powerful than ever. The demand for such an institution will never die. Humanity must always go to church to learn more of the great mysteries of life, death and conduct. When the unimportance of Christianity and the importance of the churches have been realized then the church will reshape itself to meet the needs of a wiser and a frankly un-Christian world.

But what of the importance of the clergy?

The average clergyman is attacked by his critics for being lazy and generally useless. He is maligned as a parasite and ridiculed as a sexless goody-goody. But he is what the people want him to be. So long as the people believe in Christianity, the preacher will be what he is.

The preacher is a professional friend. He aims to give advice and counsel concerning those puzzling personal problems that trouble us all. As the doctor specializes in the problems of the body and the lawyer in the diseases of the business system, so the preacher specializes in the problems of goodness. He is often as bunglesome in his treatment as the doctor and lawyer, but he will continue in his place until society obtains a substitute for him.

Philosophers and parents are the two classes of people who must be trained to take the preacher's place. And what a task! Our philosophy has entangled itself in such endless masses of verbiage that it does not even exist for the untrained thinker. Our family life is so completely broken up that the moral teachings of the home concern themselves only with traditional rudiments.

The preacher will be with us for a good many centuries to come. He gives to the masses of the people, especially in rural regions, the only philosophy they ever get. He stands out in many communities as the sole representative of education applied to moral life. His philosophy may be, probably is, a lie, but the people will cling to it until they find some one else who is intelligent enough and interested enough to give them a superior analysis of life in a way that they can understand. To them the preacher will be important until they become intelligent enough to see how little of life's secret he knows and how imperfectly human he is.

(Old Self—1974)

Since Young Blanshard wrote in the days before Billy Graham, Norman Vincent Peale, Oral Roberts and Billy James Hargis, he could have no notion of the tremendous boom in Christian salvationism promoted by these apostles of right-wing Christianity. He called such apostles in his own time "emotional calliopes who play upon the ignorance and emotional hunger of their audiences."

Some followers of Norman Vincent Peale will say that he does not belong in this company. It is true that his technique of persuasion is more restrained than that of the tent evangelists or the professional anti-Communists who use the pulpit for right-wing muckraking. He practices relatively quiet success-mongering, identifying God with Rotarian optimism. His Christ must have graduated from a Dale Carnegie Institute.

Billy Graham is more typical of right-wing evangelical Christianity. On the surface he is cheerful, suave and very, very patriotic. His handsome face has become one of the most familiar sights in American advertising, and his non-stop oratorical technique is worthy of a great auctioneer. Underneath, he is a shrewd exploiter of sin, hell, fear and sexual guilt, with a gospel very much like that of his predecessor, Billy Sunday. His published sermons constitute a lesson in marketing spiritual drugs.

"Life," he shouts, "has to be given as an atonement for sin. . . . Adam rebelled against God. His bloodstream became poisoned and every one of us as sons and daughters of Adam have blood poisoning. . . . Our Blood has been poisoned by a disease called sin. . . . You're going to die . . . and after that the Judgment. . . . I have good news! Death has been conquered. Christ is alive. He is coming back again. . . as the judge of all the earth. . . . Are you ready? . . . You and I are going to be present at the coronation of Jesus Christ when he is crowned King of the Universe."

This good news has produced more "decisions for Christ" than the pleas of any other evangelist, alive or dead. And Billy Graham's audiences have sometimes run to the half-million mark.

One reason why intelligent men should make no effort to suppress such evangelists is that, with all their false appeals to non-existent hellfire, they are nearer to primitive Christianity than many of the liberal preachers who manufacture something called Christianity in liberal pulpits. Graham, at least, appears to believe in the primitive, magical Jesus of the Resurrection and the Second Coming. If his message is incredible—and it is—it is pretty close to the message of his Master. If science should condemn one, it should also condemn the other.

Of course, the suppression of wild-eyed preaching would be worse than futile because it would destroy religious liberty, and religious liberty is one of our most distinctive possessions. Often the instrument which preserves religious liberty in our society is itself anti-rational. Jehovah's Witnesses, for example. Although this sect champions all sorts of fanaticism in medicine and education—it opposes any kind of blood transfusion even when necessary to save human life and its vision of the Pope seems to fit the legend of anti-Christ—it has been instrumental in winning more decisions for religious liberty from the Supreme Court than any other sect.

I think that our tolerance of religious oddities should apply to all types of religious fraud except those which constitute a health hazard or outright embezzlement. The exhibition of poisonous snakes at a religious service is now barred, but almost everything else in the field of religious exploitation is allowed. No law against religious fraud has ever been written that makes a workable distinction between myths that are almost true and myths that are clearly false.

The Supreme Court has rightly ducked responsibility in this murky field by declaring: "The law knows no heresy, and is committed to the support of no dogma, the establishment of no sect." And the Court since that pronouncement has gone far beyond it by removing the whole area of doctrinal disagreement from American law. It has renounced what Justice Black called "the right to measure doctrine."

In the 1940s a Los Angeles prosecutor thought he could suppress one kind of religious fanaticism by proving that it amounted to mail fraud. He prosecuted a group called "The I Am Movement," led by a Mr. and Mrs. G. W. Ballard, on the ground that they were practicing illegal deception when they claimed that their leaders shook hands with Jesus, spoke personally to George

Washington, and embodied all the good qualities of St. Germain. They also opposed liquor, tobacco, meat, onions, sex, and any use in their temple of any decorations which were colored black or red. Confronted with such an esoteric combination of idiocy and Puritanism, the Supreme Court struggled with the case for several years and finally produced a decision which amounted to a stalemate. "Men may believe what they cannot prove," said Justice Douglas for the Court, and that is where the matter stands today. Almost anything in the field of doctrine is protected as "the free exercise of religion."

If liberal critics gnash their teeth over the mindless campaigns of the praying spellbinders, they should take heart when they look back at our history and see the sharp decline of religious fanaticism over our two hundred-year history. Once citizenship rights in the American colonies were denied to those who were not Christian church members. Once dancing was rated by several Protestant denominations as an unforgivable sin. Once any defamer of the Bible could be jailed for blasphemy. Once four Quakers were hanged in Massachusetts merely for being Quakers.

Today's remarkable religious liberty in America is based in part on our blessed policy of the separation of church and state. Granted that such a phrase as "the separation of church and state" is full of difficult ambiguities—the church and the state in any society must have certain basic interrelationships—nothing in our history deserves more praise. When Jefferson and Madison sponsored the First Amendment's statement on established religion: "Congress shall make no law respecting an establishment of religion or prohibiting the free exercise thereof," few men could have dreamed that this simple pronouncement would become the basis of a broad cultural innovation in Western society. Ours had become a secular society, that is to say a society not under church control. Ours was not a Christian nation but a nation for all men, with the rights of religious dissent guaranteed. It is true that the mere adoption of the First Amendment did not at first seem to imply all these things, but the Supreme Court added these blessings to American life over the years, using the First and later the Fourteenth Amendments as launching pads for a new kind of religious neutralism in a democracy.

When we compare our fate to that of Europe, we can better appreciate the pitfalls which we have escaped. Many of the worst wars in history have occurred because of differences in faith. For many centuries, when there was the most complete union of church and state, the power of the state was used to suppress all dissent, and it was a capital offense to question seriously any major Christian dogma. Today, while there are still social penalties for religious dissent in our

society, all major laws against blasphemy have
been repealed.

It is one of the oddities of my personal history
that almost all of the great judicial battles over
the separation of church and state in our
society have been settled during the 57-year
span between Blanshard—1917 and
Blanshard—1974. I have seen American society
become a relatively neutral one in matters of
religion, and I have had the pleasure of
participating vigorously in the struggle to
achieve and preserve that neutrality. For our
final triumph in this area we have the
Supreme Court chiefly to thank, not Congress,
nor the Presidency nor the cringing state
legislatures which have yielded to sectarian
pressures. The chief heroes of the struggle
have been liberal Protestants, Jews and
unbelievers who have asserted in high tribunals
the thesis that equality of religious faiths is a
civil right and that general taxation to support
any church institution is an unlawful
establishment. In the course of the struggle the
non-Christian and the outright unbeliever have
both been elevated to the status of full
citizenship.

The high-water mark in the Supreme Court's
march to religious neutrality came in 1961 in
the case of *Torcaso* v. *Watkins.*. Roy Torcaso
was a young citizen of Maryland who wanted

to become a Notary Public. When he asked for an application blank, he saw that he was required to sign a statement professing belief in God. He was not quite certain at the time whether he believed in God or not, but he was emphatically of the opinion that his belief was none of the state's business. He believed in freedom of choice in such matters. When he was refused a license, he carried his case clear to the Supreme Court and won a unanimous decision outlawing all religious requirements for all public offices in the United States.

The Court in the Torcaso case proclaimed for the first time the full and equal rights of unbelievers. It even recognized the religious rights of those sects which do not believe in God. Said the Court: "Neither [a state nor the Federal Government] can constitutionally pass laws nor impose requirements which aid all religions as against non-believers, and neither can aid those religions based on a belief in t existence of God as against those religions founded on different beliefs." And in his decision for the Court Justice Black added: "Among religions in this country which do not teach what would generally be considered a belief in the existence of God are Buddhism, Taoism, Ethical Culture, Secular Humanism and others."

While our nation was moving toward legal religious neutrality, it was simultaneously moving toward the financial separation of church and state. The chief battle in this sector came over tax support for Catholic parochial schools. Throughout most of Europe the church had been accustomed to receiving a state subsidy for this, the most important, segment of Catholic institutional life. Even in England because of the power of the Church of England the government had endowed sectarian schools. When our thirteen colonies were established, nine of them had some form of church endowment by taxpayers.

Such endowments practically ceased for a time in the nineteenth century in the United States because of our constitutional policy of church-state separation, but with the rise of the Catholic Church as America's largest religious institution a new drive for endowment began. It came to a head with the Supreme Court's decision in the case of *Everson* v. *Board of Education* in 1947, a case in which the Court rather inconsistently allowed public money to go to sectarian schools for buses but outlawed general tax support.

The Catholic hierarchy struck back with fury, denouncing the Court's "unfair" interpretation of the Constitution, but the drift toward complete disestablishment of religion continued unabated. In 1948 in *McCollum* v. *Board of Education* the Court outlawed religious instruction in American public classrooms as an unlawful establishment of religion, and in 1962 in *Engel* v. *Vitale* and in 1963 in *Schempp* v. *School District* the Court outlawed collective prayer and collective Bible reading as parts of a religious exercise in public schools. The final blow against financial endowment for church schools came in 1973 when the Court in · *Committee for Public Education* v. *Nyquist* struck down both tax grants for tuition in sectarian schools and tax credits for parents of sectarian school pupils.

Today, although a desperate struggle is still going on over parochiaid, the major battle is won. Today the United States probably has as much religious liberty as any nation in the world, and certainly it has a more authentic and rational separation between church and state than any other large nation.

Perhaps Young Blanshard in 1917 was too arbitrary in trying to divide successful votaries of his profession into orthodox preachers who stick to their primitive Christian claims and liberals who talk themselves into believing that their own revisions and evasions constitute Christianity. Both types of preachers and priests are to some extent prostitutes of the social system in which they live, but this indictment is not as harsh or unusual as it may sound. To earn a living is a basic requirement in any society, capitalist or communist. Hence, nearly all professionals are obliged to modify their pursuit of truth in response to the social pressures exercised by the ruling class or classes. One does not have to be a Marxist or a disciple of Thorstein Veblen to acknowledge this pressure of class power.

The ideas of no class exist in purity, not even the ideas of a priestly caste. The clergyman tends to be a servant of the upper class of his society, but the same tendency is noted among doctors, lawyers and candlestick-makers. Priestly guilt seems a little more heinous than that of secular professionals because the moral claims of the priestly profession are so exalted. As Shakespeare put it, "Lilies that fester smell far worse than weeds."

My own conviction about the morals of preachers and priests is that they occupy a moral level approximating that of an advertiser of cornflakes whose showy package is about one-fourth empty at the top. The cereal manufacturer misrepresents only about one-fourth of his product. Down below the showy emptiness there is respectable substance, moral service, personal devotion and kindness. Above, there is the emptiness of all supernatural myths.

As to Young Blanshard's notions about churches which might go beyond Christianity, we will deal with such things next.

8 Beyond Christianity

(Old Self—1974)

In this last chapter I would like to turn from realities to prophecy. Prophecy, from Jeremiah to Jeane Dixon, has always been easy. The general rule is: Say what you would like to have happen and then try to twist the future to that last.

What I would like to see happen is the gradual elimination of Christianity and the substitution therefor of a rational system of moral idealism which would retain all the best

---

features of the extinct religion without losing any of its virtues.

The negative phase of my desire seems already accomplished in part. Many of the most important elements of Christianity have been eliminated before my eyes during the 57 years in which I have been first a heretic and then an outright unbeliever. The Christianity of 1974 is already a different phenomenon from the Christianity of 1917, more rational, more relevant—also more discredited.

In making an appraisal of Christianity, let us imagine that the human race had somehow come to this planet full-grown in 1974, with all the appurtenances of civilization except religion. And suppose men were given the option of choosing a religion for themselves, either Christianity or some new faith. Is it conceivable that they should pick a fragmentary religion produced in an age of antiscience and illiteracy under the misty leadership of a misty young prophet who was steeped in magic and myth, who left no systematic record of his teaching and whose vision of a Second Coming had already been contradicted by almost twenty centuries of reality? Is it conceivable that, with all modern wisdom to choose from, men would choose a religion that has been such a colossal failure in producing and permitting Inquisitions, Crusades, poverty, wars and crime? Would they not say: "Don't offer us this relic of the eras of tribalism and bloodletting? Give us something in tune with modern knowledge and the world's needs."

To come down to earth a little, let us ask certain questions about the present condition of Christianity. How much of the ancient faith can and should be saved? We may glance at the standard Roman Catholic answer, the standard and liberal Protestant answer, and the humanist answer. It may be said that by asking such questions I am bypassing the immediate, practical question: How can all branches of Christendom be united in one ecumenical movement?

Before the Second Vatican Council of 1962-65 this question had considerable weight. Earnest friends of Christian good will thought they had caught a vision of a united Christendom which would bring together a freshly accommodative Rome with a non-bigoted segment of Protestantism and a modernized Eastern Orthodoxy. A World Council of Churches was formed in 1948 with a great cluster of organizations which included almost every Christian body of importance except the papacy. And under the genial John XXIII, even the Roman Catholic Church made friendly gestures toward possible unity.

These gestures proved to be only pictorial and symbolic. Rome's idea of unity continued to be egocentric. Also, within Protestantism and Eastern Orthodoxy there appeared divisive chasms of principle and strategy. It became apparent that each branch of Christendom had prodigious vested interests at stake in the old bureaucracies. The competing schisms soon eroded "brotherhood."

Although the ecumenical movement showed progress in emphasizing social welfare, peace and racial justice, it could not heal its own theological and institutional divisions. Pope Paul's gestures of amity became cool and formal. Under his suave words of friendship he did not budge an inch from the teaching that his church had a superior status. He would not accept membership in the World Council. In spite of all the spilled words about an ecumenical world, it became apparent that the hierarchy of the Roman Church based its discussions on the old assumption that some day some time, the "separated brethren" would return to the only institution having the full sanction of Jesus Christ. Although the ecumenical movement is not yet quite dead, its leaders have turned to peripheral and non-doctrinal areas because they cannot attain any unity in the central areas of faith and power-structure.

Meanwhile, the Roman Catholic answer to the future is becoming less and less credible, and informed Catholic leaders are the first to admit this. The percentage of Catholics in the world is declining, along with a decline in creedal Christianity almost everywhere. In the United States and in Europe priests and nuns are deserting their professions in droves, and Catholic institutions are closing down in unprecedented numbers. More important, the great central doctrines of Catholicism are losing ground more rapidly among ordinary Catholics than ever before—vide the Catholic laymen's acceptance of contraception. Such ancient teachings were losing ground rapidly even before Vatican II, and the public exposure of ancient fallacies at the Council hastened the debacle.

In spite of evidence at the Council that the Catholic people wanted new teachings on birth control, celibacy, divorce and papal infallibility, Pope Paul and his associates held the fort against any substantial change in Church teaching. Even the ancient doctrine of exclusive salvation—outside the Church there can be no salvation—was modified with such ambiguity that right-wing theologians can still claim it as sacred. The *Dogmatic Constitution of the Church*, adopted at Vatican II, concedes that "many elements of sanctification and of truth can be found outside," but these elements are "gifts properly belonging" to the Catholic church.

Almost ten years have gone by since the end of the Council but until today the canon law of the church has not yielded a single important breastwork to liberal thought. Pope Paul still operates the most complete and unashamed dictatorship in the world, even more unconditional than Communist dictatorship. His assertion of divine authority still has vast political as well as spiritual significance because the Church unofficially sponsors in various parts of the world a chain of Christian Democratic parties. It also still has in leading capitals its diplomatic representatives called papal nuncios. In respect to medicine (abortion), education (parochiaid), and family law (no divorce or abortion), the semi-political church is able to operate within each country as an important right-wing force.

It is true that while the spotlights of the world were focused on the Vatican Council, the Church abandoned the regular use of the Index of Forbidden Books and it greatly relaxed the rule of Canon 1399 which forbids any Catholic to read a book directly criticizing Catholicism. But the old repressive rule is still in canon law, and its sweeping censorship provisions can still be seen in operation in Catholic universities, particularly in Catholic seminaries. Within a few weeks after the end of the Vatican Council, while the world press was still ringing with praise for the advances in religious freedom at the Council, the Apostolic Delegate in the United States—he became a cardinal shortly afterwards—summed up the Church's code for Catholic institutions of higher learning by saying: "Directly or indirectly, all studies have some connection with religion ... When there is definite teaching by the Church concerning any matter, no Catholic is free to teach differently. In like manner, it cannot be tolerated that in a

Catholic university . . . anything be taught contrary to the definitive Catholic tenets."

The "definitive Catholic tenets" include not only papal infallibility, which covers teaching on faith and morals delivered *ex cathedra* from the pope, but papal primacy, a kind of doctrinal coverall which reaches all areas of faith and binds every Catholic to accept all major papal teaching if he wants to be considered a good Catholic. Of course, there are millions of Catholic liberals in the world who risk their souls and their standing in the Catholic community by disagreeing with their pope, but they have yet to capture a single important Congregation in their Church's Curia. In June 1973, Pope Paul issued a new directive for his 4,300 bishops—all appointed by him—to refrain from publicly voicing any dissent from the pope or their fellow bishops. They should live, said the Pontiff, in a "brotherly communion of charity and obedience with the Roman pontiff."

While Catholicism will continue to lose strength throughout the world because of the advance of learning and democracy. I foresee no institutional collapse, no Catholic revolution. The love of tradition has deep roots, and Rome possesses unrivaled traditions. For many centuries to come it is likely that the papacy will continue to be one of the West's greatest bulwarks of mild conservatism, mixing decency and the love of peace with abysmal superstition and clerical exploitation of the ignorant.

This dour summary of prospective Catholic shortcomings should not lead anyone to think that Protestantism is much superior in the realm of ideas. Protestantism champions fewer fraudulent miracles than Rome, especially in the area of current production, but its over-all scheme of personal salvation through faith in the overlordship of Jesus Christ is as questionable as any Catholic saint's knucklebone, and its worship of the Bible is almost as blind as Rome's insistence on infallibility.

Protestantism's great superiority over Catholicism lies in the Protestant commitment to relative freedom of learning and relatively democratic machinery of church power. It is less static and more fluid than Rome, wherein lies its greatest strength and its greatest weakness. Also, Protestantism in the United States is committed, with few exceptions, to the separation of church and state, for which all Americans may be grateful.

I confess that in the past on many occasions I have been too grateful to Protestantism for this primarily American virtue. In platform eulogies I have echoed Luther's immortal "I can do no other" without pointing out that Luther also threw an ink-bottle at the devil, accepted most of the delusions of witchcraft and had little conception of democracy or freedom. Luther once summed up his worst principles by saying: "Universal toleration is universal error, and universal error is universal hell." Luther had been raised as a Catholic monk and some of the monastery still clung to his skirts. His pallid parallel in Geneva, John Calvin, gave at least a negative blessing to the woodpile that roasted Servetus slowly for being a unitarian, and it was Calvin's influence which kept all musical instruments out of Geneva for at least a century.

Christianity did not become wholly sane or democratic through the Reformation. It took several centuries of struggle plus the Enlightenment in Europe plus the help of Madison and Jefferson to achieve what we now call religious liberty. Protestants, of course, should not be lumped together for either praise or blame. They are disparate parts of a work force at a Tower of Doctrinal Babel. Their various leaders babble different divine messages with ambiguity and vigor.

In guessing at the future of Protestantism it might be well to separate the questions into two parts: Can fundamentalist Protestantism survive? Can liberal Protestantism survive?

Oddly enough, although I deplore all types of fundamentalism, I am inclined to give fundamentalist Protestantism a better chance of survival in the coming centuries than liberal Protestantism. This optimism (or pessimism) about the Christian future is supported by several studies that have been made recently which seem to indicate that the conservative churches of the Protestant outlook are growing more rapidly than the churches of liberal Protestantism. The solution to this riddle is not difficult to understand. When a man starts to think about realities in the absurd conglomeration called Christianity, he is not likely to stop at liberal Protestantism; he is more likely to keep on going in the direction of more complete unbelief.

Liberal Protestantism is not an easy or logical halfway house in the pilgrimage to truth. When a believer starts to break down the Apostle's Creed and says: I will accept *this* and reject *that*, the result is likely to be confusion. Nothing in the creeds seems credible when the miraculous and the mythical have been rejected. The only thing worth believing which is left is moral idealism, and Christianity has no monopoly on this product.

I think we are moving toward a more sophisticated world of moral idealism in which men will consciously write their own codes of conduct. Will they call their broadened idealism religion? I am afraid they will. The word is very, very useful for propaganda purposes and it can serve as an attractive coverall for clerical exploitation as well as moral pioneering.

I think that the idea of churches as places of sociability and moral discussion will last for a long time, and I do not deplore this. I deplore only what is being taught in those churches. I deplore it particularly because our children are being taught false concepts of life, death, salvation and goodness. They are entitled, in facing the troubled world, to know the facts of life, and today Christianity is giving them unrealities.

I regret the probable future use of the word religion to describe what should be called humanism, partly because men may use the word as an excuse for failing to speak frankly about the untruth of Christianity. That conspicuous untruth should not be perfumed away in the name of tolerance and kindness. Tom Paine was very blunt in saying in his *Age of Reason* what he thought about Christianity, and his condemnation needs to be repeated: "Of all the systems of religion that ever were invented, there is none more derogatory to the Almighty, more unedifying to man, more repugnant to reason, and more contradictory in itself, than this thing called Christianity."

Men who apply such language to *all* forms of supernatural religion have a right to describe themselves as honest humanists. This should be the first step in their attainment of integrity. They propose to take religion away from the kingdom of superstition and restore its moral values to the kingdom of man.

The humanist movement is now small and relatively weak but its strength should not be measured by membership figures. Its central ideas are spreading through the intellectual world like a fresh breeze. Many of its basic concepts were recently expressed by a new American Humanist Manifesto of 1973. Here are four key paragraphs from that Manifesto:

"We believe that traditional dogmatic or authoritarian religions that place revelation, God, ritual or creed above human needs and experience do a disservice to the human species.

"Promises of immortal salvation or fear of eternal damnation are both illusory and harmful. They distract humans from present concerns, from self-actualization and from rectifying social injustices.

"We affirm that moral values derive their source from human experience. Ethics is autonomous and situational, needing no theological or ideological sanction. Ethics stems from human need and interest. To deny this distorts the whole basis of life.

"We strive for the good life here and now."

I think we can accept this kind of humanism as a guide to the frontier that lies beyond Christianity. It must be admitted, of course, that as a word humanism is already almost as ambiguous as Christianity. There are Catholic humanists and Christian humanists and literary humanists, all trying to appropriate the humanist label. It does not belong to them. It belongs to those who assert man's independence from gods, Christs, miracles and demons. It belongs to those who battle against all the ineffable absolutes of

Christianity, scriptural or papal. It belongs to those who believe in modern man and in his infinite capacity to build an intelligent moral world for himself.

A Note on Books

There is a great deal of academic timidity and professional back-scratching in the world of Christian scholarship, and any list of significant books in this field should take into account that human condition. The standard books are not necessarily the most truthful books. Most of the so-called scholarly books about Christianity are written by men who make their living out of Christian institutions, and their enthusiasm for the institutions is not unlike that of a Florida realtor who sells waterfront lots. Too often this Christian enthusiasm is given fraternal protection by book-review editors who make a practice of assigning any book in the religious area for review to religious professionals only. It is very rare for a man on a Christian payroll to point out the obvious fact that the whole world of primitive Christianity was so waterlogged with superstition, magic and ignorance that its picture of the universe is simply unacceptable as history.

In the following short list of 22 books or sets of books worth reading, I have made no attempt to distinguish between works of so-called scholarship and competent works of propaganda. I think that the two kinds of books belong together as complements of each other. Some of the titles are out of print but can be found in good libraries.

For New Testament exegesis, Lake and Scott are sound—oddly enough, they were both professors at the two seminaries where I studied, Harvard Divinity and Union Seminary. Guignebert and Klausner are competent scholars in the Christian field; Reinach and Smith are brilliant critics of all organized religion; Mencken, Barnes and Kaufmann, particularly Kaufmann, are outstanding specialists in popular, anti-Christian scholarship. Mencken is better than his reputation.

The Hastings Encyclopedia is a factual goldmine in the whole field of religion;

Robertson is a goldmine in nineteenth-century freethought. I have included the ex-priest Joseph McCabe because I think he is important and because he has been unfairly excluded from respectable company.

If I were lost on the proverbial island and wanted three books to read in this area, I would choose Kaufmann, Reinach and Mencken.

Abbott, Walter M., S.J., *The Documents of Vatican II*. Guild Press, 1966.

Barnes, Harry Elmer, *The Twilight of Christianity*. Vanguard Press, 1929.

Blanshard, Paul, *American Freedom and Catholic Power*. Beacon Press, 1958.

Guignebert, Charles, *Christianity, Past and Present*. Macmillan, 1927.

Hastings, James, *Encyclopedia of Religion and Ethics*, 13 vols. Scribner, 1928.

Huxley, Julian, *Religion without Revelation*. Harper, 1957.

Kaufmann, Walter, *Critique of Religion and Philosophy*. Harper, 1958.

Klausner, Joseph, *Jesus of Nazareth*. Macmillan, 1925.

Jesus to Paul. Macmillan, 1943.

Lake, Kirsopp, *An Introduction to the New Testament*. Christophers, 1938.

Lamont, Corliss, *The Illusion of Immortality*. Ungar, 1965.

McCabe, Joseph, *The Story of Religious Controversy*. Stratford, 1929.

Mencken, H. L., *Treatise on the Gods*. Knopf, 1946.

Moehlman, Conrad H., *The Wall of Separation between Church and State*. Beacon, 1951.

Pfeffer, Leo, *Church, State and Freedom*. Beacon, 1953.

Phipps, William E., *Was Jesus Married?* Harper and Row, 1970.

Reinach, Salomon, *Orpheus; A History of Religions*. Liveright, 1942.

Robertson, John M., *A History of Free Thought in the Nineteenth Century*, 2 vols. Putnam, 1930.

Scott, Ernest F., *The Literature of the New Testament*. Columbia, 1943.

Smith, Homer W., *Man and His Gods*. Grosset and Dunlap, 1971.

Strauss, David F., *The Life of Jesus Critically Examined*. New York, 1970.

Wheless, Joseph, *Is It God's Word?* Wheless Publishers, 1926.